Endorsement for *Gulp*,

Brooke Boland's writing combines gentle lyricism with acute observational powers: word paintings so poetic and immersive they will take your breath away. Boland pays close attention to the world and its infinite epiphanies, both pleasurable and painful. Her essays remind us how the transcendent and the mundane are inevitably interwoven in our daily lives.

Sian Prior

Reading this book is like stumbling upon something rare in one of the garage sales Brooke Boland describes. You find yourself stunned by the rarity of the thing in your hand, and grateful that it found its way to you. This book describes the ordinary, quotidian forms of everyday life in ways that reveal the complexities of our relationships – with our world, our communities, each other and ourselves. Boland's writing is spare, yet richly infused with detail and emotional resonance. We read on, wanting to know the end of the story, but also because we know that there will be so much beauty along the way.

Natalie Kon-yu

Gulp, swallow

Brooke Boland

Brooke Boland lives and works on Yuin, Jerrinja and Wodi Wodi Country in regional NSW. She is a freelance writer and has a PhD in Contemporary Women's Writing from the University of NSW. Previously, she worked as a casual tutor, teaching writing and literature to undergraduates at UNSW and Victoria University. She works as a freelance arts writer for various publications. Her creative nonfiction has been published by *Meanjin*, *Overland*, and the *Sydney Review of Books*.

Brooke Boland

Gulp, swallow

Essays on change

First published in Australia in 2024
by Upswell Publishing
Perth, Western Australia
upswellpublishing.com

Upswell operates in the city of Perth, on ancient country of the Whadjuk people of the Noongar nation who remain the spiritual and cultural custodians of this beautiful land. We acknowledge their continuing connection to country and express gratitude to elders past and present for their strength and creativity…Always was, always will be, Aboriginal land.

This book is copyright. Apart from any fair dealing for the purpose of private study, research, criticism or review, as permitted under the *Copyright Act 1968*, no part may be reproduced by any process without written permission. Enquiries should be made to the publisher.

Copyright © 2024 Brooke Boland

The moral right of the author has been asserted.

ISBN: 978-0-645-87458-7

 A catalogue record for this book is available from the National Library of Australia

Cover design by Chil3, Fremantle
Typeset in Foundry Origin by Lasertype

Some names have been changed in these essays for reasons of privacy.

In the Nowra essay, the author and publisher acknowledge the pain and injustice meted out to children taken from their families and resettled in the UAM Home for Aboriginal Children. This was one of the first homes in NSW where 'stolen generation' children lived. We do not intend any harm in using these oral stories but rather to continue documentation of real lives that occurred through government policies and social sanction.

Contents

Newcomer	11
Death and a garage sale	17
Inferno	23
Gulp, swallow	28
No lingering traces	33
Twenty-two pairs of sunglasses	43
Rabbit person	51
Women's time	58
The leather jacket, part 1	64
Part 2	67
The death of Judy Plume	71
We can see the future	78
Why I love my chainsaw	83
Michelangelo	86
Middle-life	91
Shark	98
Milk	105
Nowra	106
Blue umbrella	115
References	119
Acknowledgements	121

I have already lost touch with a couple of people I used to be.
Joan Didion

Newcomer

In the city, no one really bothers to learn your name. My barista in the Melbourne CBD, whom I saw most days on my way to work, knew me as 'small latte' – and to me, he was 'tall barista'.

I now live in a small town two hours south of Sydney and not only does my new barista know my coffee order by heart, he also knows my name, my husband's name, my son's name, and even who my mother is. In our daily interactions, I've learned where he went to university and why he returned home to run the family café. That his partner (whose name I also know) works in the kitchen – we wave to each other, relegated as he is out the back where they never stop moving between pans and plates. All of this is satisfyingly small-town, but it is also slightly off-putting to me, someone who has until now anonymously trudged through life in metropolitan areas, where an embarrassing incident or a faux pas is quickly forgotten.

I imagine this to be the same in most places where the population falls under 4000. Towns where your new neighbour is also your husband's boss, and where a quick walk down the street leads to several friendly conversations, and you're left with the smaller half of your afternoon. If you live and work in these small towns, your neighbours are always more than neighbours – but, as I've also learned, they are always neighbours first.

'Town' – as I've called it so far – has a nice provincial ring to it. It's also a bit of a misnomer. Going into town here really means driving to Nowra, about 30 minutes up the highway, not far by regional standards. Around here we call the villages by name, necessarily shortened in the Australian vernacular: Husky, Vinny, and Sanga – Huskisson, Vincentia, and Sanctuary Point. These villages define a radius around the bay and basin that you rarely need to leave. That is, unless you need to go to Kmart, which is when you go to town.

Before moving, I lived on the outskirts of Melbourne, at the beginning of the Dandenong Ranges. My husband, who hates the cold, froze for four years, and then had enough. We were about to have a baby. Personally, I enjoyed the whiplash cold of Victoria and look back on those four years as a time when everything felt right. But when my son arrived two weeks late in September 2018, a decent 3.9 kilograms, things changed. I willingly packed up our home and moved our small family back to New South Wales. Not to south-west Sydney, where we both grew up and met in high school, but to Jervis Bay, where we had our honeymoon. We were to repeat the seachange trend: a young family, looking for a quieter life, moves to the coast.

Life lived in this small radius has given me a new appreciation of community, for both its obligations and its hospitality. You hear it everywhere – the need to 'build communities', to 'strengthen community', to 'grow communities'. But communities don't 'grow', they contract around a set of habits that are often defined by a single location and are nurtured by individuals we come to know as friends or neighbours.

Beating the tourists on sleepy weekends, it's the locals who are up and at the café by 7 am; any later and you won't get a table. It's a tight-knit group of regulars I'm introduced to the weekend we arrive. I try to learn their names but there are too many. They know all about me. They talk to my baby. They know my mother, who moved here years earlier. 'Have you found a house yet?' a woman asks (she looks familiar but I don't know her name). Everyone talks around here. A man passes through the group and stops to say hello. He walks this same street every morning, followed slowly by his old Labrador. She waddles about a block behind, resting her tired legs for a break now and then before hauling herself up to continue. Determined to get to the beach.

This area would remind many Sydneysiders of childhood vacations by the beach. In the most popular of Jervis Bay's villages, there's the ubiquitous ice cream parlour, fish and chip shop, and pub. Only now the pub has been expanded and refurbished. It gives off less of the *two-dollar-meat-raffle* vibes I remember from childhood holidays, with its questionable carpet and sticky tables. The inner-city makeover has left it almost unrecognisable, although the rough Friday night crowd remains the same. With more restaurants opening every year, two new breweries up the road, and a regular rotation of high-end retail, this little fishing village has changed dramatically. What hasn't changed are the intimate social ties that hold the community of locals together. In other words, everyone knows everyone.

With the advantage of an outsider's viewpoint, I've entered this community as an interesting social experiment, but I'm also heavily invested in my ability to integrate.

'How long does it take to become a local?' I ask the local bartender. His reply is quick, almost defensive. 'You have to live here for at least ten years.' Others say it takes two generations in the cemetery. Looks like I'm in it for the long haul. In the meantime, there are sports teams and gyms to join, photography clubs, fundraisers and volunteer opportunities, and a never-ending stream of weekend markets. I do none of these things at first. I have always been more of an observer; a writer's prerogative, I guess, although observation can only go so far. Depth, to paraphrase Helen Garner, comes from a place of connection.

Entering a tight-knit community isn't straightforward or automatic. I had an uneasy feeling of being sized up, immediately known but also unknown. This is mostly a function of curiosity with no malice behind it. Nonetheless, it's also a symptom of a divide in these small towns, tenuous and strange. Between the people who have lived here their whole life and newcomers, like me, who enter as strangers with the hope of making friends. This process can take years. But the stopover to friendship, I've learned, is becoming a regular. Which is how I met Amanda.

Amanda first made me an excellent coffee at her food truck, tucked away inside a shed that only locals knew about, and which I had recently discovered. A little bit goth, often barefoot, great taste in music. I immediately wanted to be her friend.

Every Saturday we exchanged idle coffee shop banter. I would sit outside in the sun, on pillows or crates, while Joey slept in his pram, sipping coffee and watching the locals pull up in their white SUVs to grab a quick takeaway before their kid's soccer game. Amanda's laugh would ring out in greeting, loud and untamed, often followed by a hug or kiss. She called everyone 'lover'.

'Tell me about yourself,' she said one morning. You'd hope in this moment I'd respond coolly, say something clever and off-hand. But in my self-conscious, lonely and alienated state – uncomfortably between maternity clothes and fitting back into my old jeans – came an embarrassing outpouring of detail. We realised we went to the same university, back when UNSW Art and Design was known as COFA, only a few years apart. She was a textile artist by training. We exchanged numbers and I floated home.

'Look at you, making friends,' my husband later teased.

A week later I stood on the corner, my son on my hip. An unpaid fine meant I was unable to drive home, the police officer explained, my car suddenly caught on the side of the road where he had pulled me over. There was no way to get Joey safely home in his baby seat and it was too far to walk. I needed a friend. There was only one number in my phone.

'Hey Amanda, I'm sorry to ask, but can I please borrow your car?' I explained what had happened. We barely knew each other and I was putting her on the spot. Again, I heard her laugh, this time offered in camaraderie.

'Sure, babe. Come get it.' She was only a short walk away.

Proximity and routine offer connections to people I wouldn't know otherwise, more so than in any place I have lived since childhood. In clear moments this reveals regional hospitality at its best – the generosity and willingness to lend a hand. At others, it throws into relief sharper dynamics; I know the passionate environmentalists who regularly protest over-development in our area, and I admire their cause. But I also know the group of men responsible for clearing the block of land nearby in preparation for a new housing development. How one morning, they came to work to find their equipment on fire.

Writing non-fiction from this position brings a certain risk; friends and neighbours might not like your observations, they might resent you. You might even censor yourself. If it's possible to overcome these risks, writing would likely benefit from the stimulation of these small-town dynamics. The scale it offers provides different insight into relationships and individual motivations. I'm now more interested in this detail, in people's stories rather than the news cycle, and almost unconsciously my own practice changes in response. Previously, absence had defined my approach; I preferred to write journalism, dropping the first-person pronoun and assuming a mantle of objectivity, its own subtle form of anonymity, in a way.

This doesn't mean I've settled in completely. I still bristle occasionally against the smallness of it all. I feel restless and start to crave a return to tall obnoxious buildings. Afternoons spent in galleries, followed by dinners with spilled wine and a table of friends. These moments don't last long but are regular and persistent reminders of a former life. A time before children and weekend markets. In the city, you can hold yourself separate. Relishing your own anonymity, you can move through city streets and disappear. Not here.

I try this one Friday, just for the joy of walking alone through throngs of people. It's unusually warm. The main street in Huskisson is lit with fairy lights and old-fashioned streetlamps. Several restaurants have tables pulled out onto the walkway. I admit it's a short walk. I'm stopped a few times for a quick chat. Wave and shout hello to some casual acquaintances and friends out with their families for an early dinner. There's no anonymity here. I return home via the drive-through bottle shop, have a yarn at the register, defeated in my attempt to disappear but not disappointed. Driving with the casual abandon that comes with well-known local roads, wine and beer jostling on the front passenger seat, music turned up, I realise it has been a long time since I felt this way. Like I was home. It only took two years.

Published *Sydney Review of Books*, 2022

Death and a garage sale

'I died last year,' he said. We stood in the front yard of his house, thrown together by the suburban ritual known as the garage sale. It was his house, his yard, his stuff. The cast-offs of his life spread across the lawn and being picked over by neighbours and strangers.

I wore my one-year-old son, Joey, on my hip as we talked, his small body wriggling impatiently. Joey's unrelenting appetite for things – objects, people – took over. I put him down and he shuffled between cardboard boxes and discarded pots and pans, wobbling on two legs. This was our weekly habit. I got up early Saturday morning, dressed Joey and headed out. I never had an idea of what I was looking for, only that I'd know it when I see it. But today it looked like it might rain, and there was nothing here that interested me. I only lingered to hear the rest of this stranger's story, his quiet tale of resurrection on a hard table in a Sydney hospital.

He'd had a few heart attacks. Too stressed, too busy, he explained.

'A few?' I asked.

'Three.'

It was the third attack that stopped his heart. Afterwards, he sold off his chain of pharmacies, his family home, and moved here to the coast.

As he spoke he scratched at the new hair on his chin. He had begun to grow a beard, stiff and white.

In a way, his motivations for moving here were similar to my own. My husband and I left the city to find a slower pace. I wanted more time with my son, and we both wanted to be closer to family. One year on, though, I had grown familiar with the stiffening of my jaw, closely followed by a physical need to get outside. An inability to breathe deeply enough. These feelings never lasted long but had become more frequent.

Joey interrupted us with his busyness. He was removing items from one box and putting them in another, clucking to himself. Linens and kitchen utensils – cutlery, pillowcases – found themselves strangely paired. I moved everything back quickly as the man walked away to help another punter. What was he hoping to find here on the coast? Peace and quiet? We headed back to our car empty-handed just as it started to rain. Joey threw his head back, felt the drops fall against his cheeks, and laughed.

The longer I watch the small body of my child grow, the more I realise how quickly life moves. The small, intimate demands of child rearing have become a lesson in my own impermanence.

When, about a year after that day at the garage sale, I am lying in my son's bed with a pile of books to read before sleep, neither of us are the same person. He selects one and demands to read it himself, flexing his newfound independence. I linger uninvited, understanding this is how it should be.

I find myself thinking about the resurrected man. I never asked him what it was like to die. Some people describe it as slipping into peaceful quiet blackness, others see gardens, or loved ones long deceased – a sign that perhaps our body gives way before our consciousness loosens. If I believed in reincarnation, this would be the moment before rebirth, when the soul passes from one body to another. Except I don't believe in anything. Perhaps this is the problem: a determined lack of faith, a failure of belief. Mortality is more predictable, finite in its required materiality and recognition of our body changing as time flies.

I mark time by the few short years of my son's life as he reaches each milestone.

Turning one,

Two,

and then

Three.

On each of his birthdays I chart his height religiously in black marker as he stands with his back against his bedroom wall, touching his heels lightly against the kickboard, wanting desperately to grow. This is my own supplication, too. A prayer of hope and thanks.

'There, look at that! You've grown so much.' I show him a finger-width of time.

After lockdowns, we return to our Saturday morning routine. One time we follow the handmade cardboard signs to a two-storey home that sat high above the street and was wrapped by a single veranda. Below the house was a garden of overflowing green palms with a steep climb to the garage. An older woman, tall and thin, had opened the roller doors and laid out the belongings of her late husband along the driveway. It was a memento mori of woodworking tools and unused timber.

'Would you like to choose a toy? It's free.' She offers us a basket of toys her grandchildren used to play with when they visited. Joey shyly selects a set of fairy wings while I poke through old gardening tools. I never know what I'm looking for, only that I know it when I see it.

When we wave goodbye, she stands at the top of the driveway above it all, cradling a hot cup of tea in her hands. It was delivered to her by a woman who looked like a daughter, their heads bending slightly towards each other in private communion.

One night my son and I read a book, and there is a word he's never heard before: heaven.

'Who is heaven?'

'It's actually a place. Some people believe it's where people go when they die.' I leave it there.

It's only a few months later when our old dog doesn't come back from a visit to the vets. I return home with only her collar on the car seat next to me. As I pull up in our driveway, for the first time in a long time, the bins haven't been knocked over. I don't have to put rubber gloves on and pick up the garbage while she stands grey-faced, guilty, at a distance. I can't breathe. Who's going to eat all Joey's crusts now?

For a week, my son tells everyone about his dead dog, Harley. One well-meaning friend says she's gone to heaven – making him pause.

'When will she come back?'

From there, his questions drop one after the other.

'Will we live forever?'

'Will I die?'

'When will you die, Mum?'

I watch him on the swing as he tips his small body over its centre and spins and spins.

'Mum, I don't want to die like Harley did.'

Again, later that night as I tuck him into bed. 'Mum, I don't want to die.'

Each time he says this, I offer him the same line: we will all live long, happy and healthy lives together. What else to say to a child? That we never know what tomorrow will bring?

Children; we watch the hypnotic up down of their chest when they sleep, the small fluttering at their throat, and find ourselves making impossible promises: Nothing bad will ever happen to you; I will always be here; you will never be alone.

Suddenly, the questions about death stop. We become preoccupied with other important things, like what will be in his lunchbox.

'Mum, what am I eating today?' He drags his small wooden chair over to the kitchen bench and climbs up.

'A sandwich, yoghurt, strawberries.' The last always cut in half in fear of needles.

'Pickles, and a banana,' I say as I continue making his lunch. He inspects the items.

'But what will I put in the afternoon tea bowl?'

We decide on the banana, which will sit comfortably in the bowl for the day without spoiling.

Every morning he checks his lunch box. His biggest concern in life is not having a snack suitable for the afternoon tea bowl, like the other children.

The question begins to haunt me.

As I fall asleep at night: What will go in the afternoon tea bowl?

As soon as I wake up: What will go in the afternoon tea bowl?

When I buy the groceries: What will go in the afternoon tea bowl?

I never know what I'm looking for, only that I know it when I see it: Sultanas in small cardboard boxes, mandarins, miniature bags of popcorn. I imagine Joey choking and put the popcorn back.

The afternoon tea bowl needs to be fed daily. It is ravenous with hunger. It is growing, like the body of a small child desiring to fit in.

Meanwhile, I've been neglectful; my own afternoon tea bowl is empty. It has plenty of peace and quiet, but it can't live on those. I put in work, new furniture, more work. I become preoccupied with other important things and act like we're going to live forever.

Inferno

It's over a year ago now that I watched from my parents' garden as the sky turned a deeper, dirtier red. The birds were gone, replaced by camps of bats silhouetted black as they circled above us, confused and disorientated. The next morning, we saw Lake Conjola devastated on the news. My cousins cut our New Year celebrations short, quickly packed their things, and left. The highway clogged with escaping tourists.

Our small seaside village on the south coast of New South Wales suddenly fell quiet. The day before I had struggled to find a parking spot, driving in circles around Huskisson. Now only a few of us locals remained, committed to getting on with our routines as the smoke cleared briefly. At the chemist the regulars made conversation. Leave or stay? An old woman admitted quietly that she had no car and nowhere to go anyway. She was on her own, like so many.

Others were confident and waved away any concerns. Then the roads closed and how everyone felt didn't really matter any more. Either way we were stranded. A man in high-vis and steel-capped boots – only here for a day's work – wandered up and down the main street, not going anywhere, unsure whether to book a night at the local motel. This was our limbo, the first circle of hell, dark and deep and hopeless. Only it wasn't fog, as Dante described. It was smoke.

We had moved here eight months earlier, looking for a sea change, and purchased a tiny cottage perched on a hill, surrounded by five acres of thick bushland. Idyllic. A lyrebird to keep us company. Now home felt like a trap. There was really only one way in and out, and it happened to be the Princes Highway, the same arterial road that was jammed with traffic from further south – and then suddenly closed.

The day they reopened the highway we packed as much as we could into the car and dropped everything off at my parents' house in the suburbs nearby. A favourite pair of jeans, some of my son's toys, photo albums, my grandmother's wedding ring. This unfamiliar feeling (despair, perhaps) in the pit of my stomach as my husband and I tripped back and forth from the house with armloads of bags and bits and pieces – a jumbled assembly of family life.

This happened three times over several days. The fires came closer each time and continued to behave erratically. The second time the tourists were evacuated. The third time emergency services warned residents to be prepared, and we left for Sydney. We returned a few days later to find the edges of the neighbouring property smouldering, a few kilometres from our small weatherboard cottage. We drove to the top of the hill to see the fire soft and low – nothing like the images we'd been bombarded with for weeks. This fire had burnt for seventy-four days and now it was petering out nearby. I watched from our kitchen window each morning as the smoke curled from the tree line below. While we waited, our son collected blackened gum leaves from the lawn and we started reorganising our home; we unpacked the bags, had our tanks emptied and cleaned. The water contaminated by smoky run-off and now undrinkable.

That summer seems long ago now. At the time I couldn't write it down. I read accounts by people who experienced the fires and those in cities affected by poor air quality and had a writer's guilt that I should be part of the conversation. But there was only time for packing and waiting. And waiting meant listening to the radio for regular updates, making sure we had enough food and water in case the highway closed again, triple-checking our house insurance details. I was exhausted by the waiting.

Exhaustion, I suppose, was only one reason why I didn't write. Well, I did write: the tireless grind of copywriting for money. That I could manage easily enough, with a mercenary attitude. But here was *something* to write about. It was like looking through a dirty window unable to make out the view; I couldn't write a word. Iris Murdoch experienced a similar sense of disconnection. 'I have a very shallow mind and I've been skating round these last four years on the crust of it,' she writes in a letter to Frank Thompson, dated 1943. This was how I felt at the time, skating on the crust of it all.

In between the packing and the waiting, nothing made sense. I turned to description instead, struggling at the time to move beyond observation to any deeper understanding. I took notes of shop owners standing out the front of empty stores, staring at the sky; Dad hosing the ash off my car as his grandson watched, fascinated, like all children, by hoses; trees with alien regrowth barely recognisable as trees. I'm unable to pull these images into anything more than vignettes. I take no deeper meaning from them, there's no larger plot to hang them off. And without physical access to a space where writing and thinking happens, routine evaporated.

In the month following the summer fires, I returned to my part-time marketing job. This was an hour-long drive away, involving lengths of dirt roads. At any moment a wombat or kangaroo might emerge. It's a beautiful but isolated area and it didn't fare well during the Currowan megafire. We, my colleagues and I, were warned about the destruction along the main access road before we returned. Some of us chose to drive in together, a slow morning convoy through charred bushland, vast in its emptiness, appearing as if larger and deeper now that it was stripped of life. Before, in every leaf and animal, this place hummed. Now stark and empty, it was overwhelming on a different scale. Everything familiar replaced by a still and quiet landscape.

It was different at home, where nature suddenly became unruly. A second male lyrebird moved onto our property, challenging the established bird's dominion. They battled through song – all day, they sang. We could hear them from every corner of the house, mimicking birdsong. But they do more than copy. With every imitation each bird adds something all his own, a flourish, an ending, a lilting – ahahaha. They steal from the kookaburras and the black cockatoos, but I don't think the other birds mind. They quietly watch his shaking, bowing body as he sways beneath them, tail curled tightly above his back, hearing an echo of themselves against the canopy. Perhaps in this painstaking imitation they find something new as well.

Six weeks after the threat of fire passed, our thin tin roof gave way, and the water came down the walls and dripped from light fittings. The river in town rose overnight and higher again the next day. It felt like the rain we had prayed for over summer was falling at once. Nature laughed at us. You wanted rain? Well, here it is. Someone joked that next we'd have a plague. Then came cicadas so loud we had to take our phone calls inside, and even then, people commented on the noise, asking whether the line was bad. This happens every nine years or so, a neighbour informed us, when several generations of cicadas emerge simultaneously from the ground.

The millipede invasion arrived with the pandemic. These creatures were denied their usual nocturnal behaviour and turned up everywhere. You can't kill them because that only brings more, to feast on the crushed bodies. I learned to sweep each one up carefully and quickly throw them into the garden, my son delighting in the tight balls of their bodies. Suddenly both my husband and I were home, fighting for space and time as our two-year-old demanded more of us. My capacity for work halved, and then halved again, because more time at home only means more housework and caring responsibilities. One day, as I hung another load of washing on the line, I heard a crunching sound. No one else was around. *Crunch*. I looked up, into the trees. A large flock of glossy black cockatoos, birds I only usually saw from a distance, quietly crunching gum nuts in the trees above my head, watching me.

These sudden arrivals and infestations were our small private challenges when social distancing separated us from work and family. Still, the distance was almost welcome, at least at the beginning. I no longer had to drive through scorched bushland or check if roads had been washed away. Instead, I attended Zoom meetings via a 3G internet connection, technology that has been outdated for over ten years. The trees, transformed by fire, began to grow outwards instead of up, and the rest of Australia seemed to forget about what had happened here.

Somewhere within it all the words started to come back. So slowly at first, I barely noticed, then suddenly like a flood. I wrote every morning and began to feel more at ease. In hindsight, it was grief that opened up the gates. The private grief that came with pregnancy loss. It lifted the fog that had descended at the time of the summer fires as I wrote to understand.

When the fires came through the danger was too immediate. I couldn't write about it because I couldn't see it from any distance. I was too close and looking back now, I understand that at the time of its unfolding, catastrophe refuses representation in its immediacy. That comes later, once the threat passes. Retrospect conceives the example we later use to understand what's happened and, hopefully, this allows us to learn from it. How we represent these events can begin to normalise these experiences, covering up the exhaustion and the fear. It never felt normal, though, not even for a second. This is how things, events, become reflections of themselves in an estranged way, as hindsight.

Now I can say it was smoke, not fog, as Dante wrote. I can remember the man wandering in high-vis and place him in this story as a lost soul. But at the time, I only noticed he looked as tired and confused as I felt, in his heavy boots, stranded in a town that held a garden hose as hope, bats circling overhead.

Published *Sydney Review of Books*, 2021

Gulp, swallow

I'm sitting on the verandah with my father, not looking at the view. He's sick, with the kind of condition you don't know you'll come back from. One end of a line runs directly to his heart, the other end dangles from under his arm. His distinguishing feature – a moustache – is gone. What's left of his hair is thin and shaved short against his skull. His head is back, his eyes are closed against the sun.

We sit this way for a while in companionable silence, something I've come to recognise as a disposition – genetics, or something else – that I've inherited from him, a need for company without the talking. We all know what will happen next week: he'll get a call to go back to hospital for a second round of chemo; I'll self-consciously slip socks and shoes on his knotted feet and tie up his laces; noticing his ankles, one replaced years earlier and still swollen, the other surgically fused to stop the pain of bone rubbing bone. For three weeks or maybe longer, he'll be confined to four hospital-grey walls with a window that won't open, and no visitors allowed.

If we did speak in this moment, if we said what we were feeling, it would be too much. We would crack open, and nothing could stop the outpouring of love and fear and grief once it started. Afterwards, we'd never forgive ourselves. Just to sit for a while in the sun with each other nearby was enough.

'Did you hear about the new dinosaur they've discovered in the UK?' Dad asks. His eyes are open. *Pendraig milnerae*. Found in a limestone quarry in the 1950s, the four perfectly preserved 250-million-year-old fossils were mistaken for crocodilian remains and filed away, waiting in the wrong drawer for years. This is a conversation we can have.

My son, a three-year-old palaeontologist, is inside lining dinosaurs up in pairs. His arrangement mimics family relationships – mother and child, sister and brother. I survey the Cretaceous period re-created in miniature across my parents' living room floor and ask Joey to pack up his toys. *Triceratops, Pachycephalosaurus, Ankylosaurus.* We are on the Gondwana coast. Sea levels rise quickly, leaving an 80-kilometre stretch of Wandrawandian siltstone behind, from Gerroa to Kangaroo Valley to Ulladulla, while we go further underwater. In a few million years, an asteroid the size of Mars will slam into earth, pushing it further off its axis and bringing darkness to the planet while volcanic eruptions – the stuff of nightmares – will release dangerous levels of carbon dioxide, enough to kill 80 per cent of what's left on earth. But back in the Anthropocene, I can see dad is getting tired and it's time to go home.

My early memories of him are more like sensations: his teeth a curiosity that sat on the bedside table at night; the overwhelming smell of spilt coffee and beer in his work ute; his moustache always prickly and tickling; and the way he made me hold a small hand over his eyes to block the light as he dozed on the lounge of an evening. 'I'm just resting my eyes,' he'd say, and my brother and I would wait for his heavy snoring to start, immediately changing the channel to the cartoons that were banned in our house.

As a child, Dad would stand out the front of the pub at Catherine Hill Bay with his pet goat, singing the theme song to *Davy Crockett* for a free soft drink, his father somewhere inside. He was about four years old. This is a story I heard from Mum. The truth is Dad rarely speaks about these things. On the few occasions I've asked, his answers are brief, arriving in short staccato.

His mother, who hated the sound of the waves at night, led the family's move to Blacktown, where they built a house on Flushcombe Street with the help of a war service loan. Their father, who had terrible arthritis in his hands and died young from kidney failure, was a police officer. During the school holidays Dad would work at Riverstone Meatworks for £5 a day. Later he became a builder, then a glazier, spending the rest of his life working on the high rises now dominating Sydney's skyline. I remember standing on the footpath in the city as a small girl, holding Mum's hand while we craned our necks trying to find him, staring up at the men suspended 12 storeys in the air on the side of a building, small specks moving in the distance. Strangers joined us on the ground, glaring up into the sun, wondering what we were pointing at.

A builder by trade and habit, he was always making something and built our family home, an oversized four-bedroom brick house in south-west Sydney, over the course of my childhood. When I was instructed to take a glass of ice water out to him or call him in for lunch, I'd find him near the shed with a builder's pencil or screw held in one corner of his mouth. He'd scull the water as if he were dying of thirst and ignore me the rest of the time. At the end of the day, he'd stand with a foot perched above his knee, in blue King Gee shorts, balancing on one leg and leaning against the kitchen bench. The only time I ever saw him sit down was when the cricket or football was on. When I look in the mirror, I see his dark hair and skin and eyes, his frown.

He built this house too, where my parents now live; a monolith of glass and concrete sitting at the point where the mouth of Currambene Creek opens into the bay. This is the place to watch an unfolding comedy of errors at the whim of its perennial tide. Boats are regularly trapped on the sandbank. Tourists attempting a reflective paddle downstream on a board or in a kayak are held in place, as if on a treadmill, not moving an inch no matter how fast they work their arms. The likelihood of reaching the shoreline opposite disappears quickly. Predictably, the water returns with bream and flathead and white trevally. Boats are saved, people float home.

Today it's the welcome swallows that catch our attention. They cartwheel nearby, feathered acrobats twisting in the air, dramatically close to the fence. These red-throated, delicate birds appear at the beginning of spring, a sign of warming weather and changing seasons. In their circular and graceful theatrics, full pelt chasing down midges, they are collectively known as a gulp (of swallows) and their light bodies can reach speeds up to 65 kilometres per hour. Helped along by evolutionary design, their tails are deeply forked to create the kind of drag needed to bank sharply.

I hear a dull *thuck* as the first swallow hits the glass, making my father look. *Thuck* – a second bird lies motionless on the hot timber deck. In the middle of their acrobatics, two swerved headfirst into the glass sliding door. The humans on the verandah spring into action; we open all the doors and line up chairs in a row outside, a hopeful deterrent. Mum moves the small bodies into the shade and we wait to see if they are simply stunned. My son can't take his eyes from them. Will they come back to life? One swallow moves a little and sits up. A moment later it rejoins the others in the air and we all cheer. The second swallow is still and quiet, his neck clearly broken. The gulp continues its spin.

When Joey and I return a few hours later, Dad is sitting up in bed wearing a red woollen beanie and winter coat on a 20-degree afternoon, watching TV. He changes the channel – cartoons – and Joey climbs in with his grandpa. 'We still need to bury that swallow,' I say to no-one in particular, looking out the window. A single magpie sits on the roof, waiting for Mum to throw small lumps of mince onto the grass.

Birds are one of the last surviving signs of dinosaurs. Their smaller avian form descended from carnivorous theropods such as the velociraptor and tyrannosaurus rex. If you ever look a caged brahma rooster in the eye, his feet as big as your fist, you'll see the family resemblance. Propped up impossibly on two legs with talons, it is small-brained and feathered, aggressive. When some dinosaur species started shrinking at incredible rates and refining wing design, it sparked a sudden evolutionary change that led to the modern bird. Sudden, in evolutionary time, meaning millions of years. Only it hasn't stopped there. Swallows, some say, are getting smaller, shortening their wingspan to protect themselves from cars, of all things. I wonder if they ever think about avoiding windows.

'This one is dead,' I explain to Joey, who is now crouched over the bird, still waiting for it to spring back to life. When I look at my son, I see the same dark hair, same frown. But he has his father's eyes. 'We need to dig a hole and bury it in the ground.'

I don't go with them as Mum takes his hand and heads downstairs to the garden. While she digs a shallow grave, I stay upstairs with Dad. It's Joey who is left gently holding the soft dead body in both hands, contemplating its feathered form, trying to understand the ritual of a burial. After a short funeral, he stares at the dirt for a good minute. 'It will jump up out of the ground and fly off with the others,' he insists.

When Mum tells me this story later, I immediately reach for a touchstone I can offer his young mind. 'You know how dinosaurs were hit be an asteroid and turned to bone? The bird you buried will stay in the ground and become bones. It won't come back to life.' Joey just shrugs and gets on with things. Timelessness is the free-ranging territory of young children, unhindered as they are by adult concerns. Almost a week later, I overhear a conversation between Joey and his dad about a bird that's in the ground, like a dinosaur, that won't come back to life. 'It's very sad,' Joey says, leaning against the chair, a foot perched above his knee, balancing on one leg.

Published *Meanjin*, Winter 2022

No lingering traces

When I drive, I'm reminded of things my mind has closed a curtain over. This time, a hot, angry march up the long driveway of my childhood home. The items in my backpack carefully selected – a favourite toy and seven pairs of underpants. I was running away. But by the time I reached the road, all resolve had left my body; I'd realised there was nowhere to go. I turned and headed to our backyard. Then hid up a tree for an hour hoping Mum would start to worry. That would show *her*. How she laughed that night when she unpacked the bag and found the seven pairs of underpants folded at the bottom. One for every day of the week, I explained.

The last remaining agricultural footholds and hobby farms outside Sydney flashed past. A few more hours and we'd be closing in on the heart of Wonnarua Country, where mining is still the largest employer and vineyards dominate the local tourist brochures. From there, it's not far to the farm where my aunty lives. A small operation in Baerami, a name long associated with oil shale and a town cut through by the Goulburn River.

That day, driving north, I was sore and emotional. The release of prolactin and oxytocin – my body's way of making me feel good when I nursed my baby – suddenly dropping now I had stopped breastfeeding my son. My breasts were two stones misplaced on my body. I was unable to raise or lower my arms without pain, so I gripped the steering wheel awkwardly, hunched, elbows out. Breastmilk soaking through another shirt. It would take two weeks before the milk would dry up, and another six months before my bone density would return to normal. I probably smelt bad. I didn't care. In other words, as far as travelling companions went, I was a delight.

In another year, I would be diagnosed with post-natal depression and anxiety, which gave me a tidy name that defined this time in my life – the way diagnoses often label experience neatly. I felt desperate. The endless fogginess, the gutted feeling that I hadn't slept in months.

Mum sat in the front passenger seat. Her eyes closed, breathing heavily. She wasn't asleep, she just hated the bends. This was how she got through it. I drove slowly down the single-lane road as it wound tightly between two national parks. On one side, impressive rock walls, on the other a sudden drop into deep gullies that had been gutted by recent bushfires. This old road was once a government secret, built as an escape route from Sydney to the Hunter Valley during the Second World War. A road for running away. In the backseat my two-year-old son, Joey, was asleep, his little head falling forward. I trained the rear-view mirror on him and kept one eye there.

The endless rows of burnt trees were regrowing their green leafy fuzz, alien branches sprouting from trunks. Occasionally a house appeared between them, a survivor. But the crumpled outbuildings and sheds closer to the road hadn't fared as well.

'Some houses are still standing,' Mum said, her eyes open now. I grunted in response. She had been there at my last doctor's appointment, after I didn't sleep for a week and grew frantic. I had sat at her feet in my living room while she combed the knots from my dirty hair.

'Do you think of hurting yourself or your baby?' the doctor had asked me.

'No.'

I didn't tell him how every day was blunt. He gave me a referral for another blood test and said to come back in a month.

We arrived at my aunt's house during a late lambing season, just after a farmers' warning was issued. The unusually cold weather meant many newborn lambs, and some adult sheep, were freezing to death overnight on farms across New South Wales. Aunty Marl told us how she found their small bodies frozen on the hard ground each morning, the mothers standing nearby. While she viewed these little deaths with empathy, she also maintained an emotional distance that comes with life on a farm, where death is everywhere and shooting something weak is its own kind of mercy. Today, one ewe and her newborn lamb were in the field near the house where she could keep an eye on them. This mother had given birth to twins a few days earlier. Only the one at her feet – small even for a newborn lamb, with shaky, weak hind legs – had survived. We didn't like his chances.

Aunty Marl could calm a horse with just her voice and always looked right in hat, gloves, and boots. After her divorce forty years earlier, she sold the family home in Sydney and moved her two kids to the country. I'd never told her this, but I admired her independence. She now had the farm and country house she wanted, along with a new partner, Joe, who learnt how to farm from his father and had made his money in chickens. Now 'retired', they raised a few sheep. But Joe's passion was always for birds. Every morning he fed the small finches and doves that visited and built nesting boxes for all of them. He released pigeons in distant places to see how long it would take for them to fly home. He could identify every bird on his land, sometimes with the help of his bird book, which sat like a bible on the kitchen bench.

The sheep and birds weren't the only residents. The property still operated as a chicken farm, with several large steel sheds, now managed by someone else. Eggs were collected daily and moved into the hatchery at one end of the farm, away from the house. Hundreds of hatchlings emerged weekly.

That afternoon, Joe offered to show us inside on of the chicken sheds. I held Joey on my hip as we slid open the heavy door to the shed and watched the day-old chicks scatter.

A wave of heat from the constant overhead lamps hit us as we stepped inside.

'Keep quiet and move slowly,' big Joe instructed.

Too much noise and these tiny bodies would panic, rushing into a crowded pile, suffocating and crushing one another in a mass of tiny yellow fuzz.

A farmhand was already in the shed, bent over with arms outstretched. She moved low and slow across the sawdust floor as she gently drove the chicks to the other end of the shed. As she moved, she collected tiny limp bodies as she found them.

'There's always a few that don't survive,' big Joe said, offhand. The stale, hot air inside the shed was oppressive and I suddenly felt nauseous. I moved back towards the door to leave, and little Joe twisted in my arms as he watched the wave of yellow starting towards us.

A few days into our visit we had a new routine. My son and I took the UTV out for a lap of the property each morning, which was like go-carting but with more purpose. First, we released the dogs from their crates, racing them behind the chicken sheds before veering into the fields. Grass parrots shot out in front of us as we made tracks across the damp morning grass, heading for the sheep to see if any more were born overnight. Then a quick check on the older lambs too, and a visit to Aunty Marl's chickens – a more fortunate group of hens than those in the sheds.

We peeked into their laying boxes, and Joey excitedly held an egg in each hand. But we also found one egg smashed. This repeated for a few days until we realised one hen had developed a taste for egg.

It became our mission to catch her in the act. Finally, we saw her early one morning. A fat brown bird with egg on her face. I herded Egg-face into a corner and locked her up separately. Then I told big Joe we'd caught the culprit.

'What are you going to do with her?' I asked him.

'She's dinner,' he replied. He was joking. Maybe.

'She won't peck the eggs if she can't see,' he added confusingly.

I followed Joe to his work shed and watched as he rummaged through a drawer. He held up a tiny pair of bright orange goggles. Chicken goggles. I watched in surprise as he held Egg-face between his legs and fastened them expertly above her beak. Like a tiny set of blinkers.

'These animals aren't pets,' Joe reminded me one day. 'They're livestock.'

There's a difference here that I tried to understand as we rounded up the sheep and Joe worked the dogs. The semantic inference is one of distance; pets you're allowed to love, but livestock are an asset. Livestock can be farmed and sold without a second thought. This is how language reveals its emotional baggage.

'What about your dogs?' I asked.

We watched the two Koolies – Peach and Tiggy – as they moved forward instinctively and pushed the sheep through the paddock toward the gate. One short whistle from Joe, and they dropped back, almost disappearing into the long grass. The dogs never took their eyes off him, or the sheep in front.

'They're working dogs.' Emphasis on *working*.

So not pets.

'TIGGY, get back,' he shouted.

Naming had a purpose too.

I decided to love them anyway.

Tiggy was my favourite. Her back right leg was permanently bent from an accident when she was a puppy. She often hopped as she ran alongside the UTV or chased the sheep, but it didn't slow her down. She went hard on the sheep, a little too hard.

'She would be better off working cattle,' Joe said.

After the sheep were moved and the work was done, I found Tiggy out the back lazing in the sun near the verandah. She saw me, became all legs and tongue and wriggling body. I whispered to her that she could come home with me if she wanted, where I would let her sleep inside, and we could go for walks. Even as I said it, I knew it was a cruel invitation. There's nothing worse than a working dog that doesn't get to work.

The newborn lamb we'd met on our first day was becoming stronger and bumbled around by his mother's side. In the mornings, when we delivered feed to the mother, she came running. But the lamb hung back, bleating nervously from a distance. One morning big Joe said it was time for them to join the other sheep in the far paddock with more feed. We took them over in a convoy of dogs and UTVs and watched as they met up with the rest of the flock.

Lambs, it turned out, are hilarious. There were about thirty in this flock, and every morning you could see them jumping and prancing in pirouettes. Then they fell into exhausted woolly piles alongside their mother's legs. When they woke an hour or so later, it was chaos. You could hear them from the house. Their frantic bleating, a chorus of lambs calling loudly for their mums, who had mindlessly grazed further and further away while they slept. The flock became a disordered jumble of woolly bodies and endless high-pitched calls until just as suddenly it fell quiet.

I was tired and lay next to my son as he napped. We slept like this for two hours. When I woke up, my mother laughed that I was always tired lately.

'Maybe you're pregnant,' she joked.

I sat on the toilet holding a pregnancy test in one painfully raised hand and waited for the result. It took seconds for the bright blue plus sign to appear.

'Oh, SHIT.'

Then I laughed. Breastmilk leaked through another shirt.

When Joey and I returned home from the farm two weeks later I visited my doctor, who confirmed the news.

'Are you taking pre-natal vitamins?' she asked.

'Yes.'

'Do you know when your last period was?'

'No.' I hadn't had a period for almost two years.

She sent me for an ultrasound. On the day, I was the expectant mother, waiting for a glimpse at the small life taking shape inside her body. My husband, Danny, came with me, now less shocked and accepting that this was happening. Suddenly, there it was on the screen, a tiny cluster of cells. Its frantic heart beating.

When we got home Danny stuck the sonogram high on the fridge with the Spider-Man magnet that had followed us from house to house over the last ten years. Names were suggested and discarded, a friendly disagreement that would never be settled until the baby arrived; we both knew that. It was nice to imagine our baby for a moment and we talked excitedly for the first time. I liked Rose for a girl.

I woke with sharp pain and heavy bleeding. Danny was at work in the shed.

'I can't take you to the hospital, I have three more clients.' He dismissed me.

I packed my son's nappy bag, popped two Panadol, and headed for Emergency.

'I'm having a miscarriage,' I told the receptionist while trying to stop Joey from touching the glass partition.

She gave me a form to fill in.

'A bit of bleeding doesn't mean you're having a miscarriage,' she said as I returned it. I was just another anxious pregnant woman appearing at her window. I said something about a lot of blood. She told me to take a seat.

Three hours later the sonographer pressed down on my stomach while my son stood beside the hospital bed crying, holding my hand. Neither of us sure of what was happening. No-one at the hospital said the word 'miscarriage' – not before or after – but it was there in her discreet silence as she searched. There was nothing on the screen. I walked out of the hospital with the cannula still in my arm.

The rest of the week was a jumble of doctors' appointments, blood tests, phone calls. An internal ultrasound was required to make sure nothing was left. I called four clinics before I found one with an available appointment that wasn't weeks away. The receptionist listed instructions with detachment. *11:50 empty bladder. Between 11:50–12:20 drink 800 mls of water. 1:20 appointment.*

On the day, I sat in the waiting room facing a tactless poster that asked, 'Are you pregnant?' and suggested vitamins. Most of the women were here for an ultrasound with their partners, couples excited for a peek at their unborn child and the sonogram they'd soon hang on their fridge. My first sonogram had revealed a small white smudge surrounded by shadow and was still held in place on the fridge by Spider-Man, his magnetised hands clinging to the white metal.

Before long a woman called my name, and I followed her along the hallway to a small dark room. We were both using the word 'foetus' now instead of 'baby' – which was accurate, correct, scientific, as it should be in these moments, I suppose. Like the difference between pets and livestock, we created the distance with words.

As I lay there, she pushed down painfully on my bladder for a while and then directed me to the bathroom, so I could pee and change my pad before the internal exam. I found myself facing yet another pregnancy poster, this time on the back of the toilet door; the silhouette of a happily pregnant woman, one hand on her stomach – a gesture of maternal fulfilment – surrounded by sunflowers.

I had put this ultrasound off for days, hoping the bleeding would stop before it had to be done. It hadn't. If you've ever been required to lie down for thirty minutes while someone examined inside you, then you already know how uncomfortable this is. When you cry in this position, the tears end up in your ears. Unlike the sonographer at the hospital, this woman didn't pass me the tissues. Her tongue clicked, then she remarked that the ultrasound looked clear – 'no lingering traces'.

I called a friend currently locked down in Melbourne. I felt guilty. Guilt at my ambivalence in the early days of pregnancy; that I did something wrong. And angry too because no one had believed me when it happened, not even my husband. She was kind and generous, her sympathy genuine and advice helpful. Then she told me she had five miscarriages after the birth of her only daughter.

'You make your peace with these things,' she said. 'Sometimes life is just out of our control.' The gentle practice of acknowledging life for what it offers, and not what it withholds, peeking through.

A few weeks later, Danny and I stood in the kitchen and yelled at each other the way people hurting sometimes do. Suddenly, I was desperate for his promise that we'd try again. He couldn't give it.

'I don't even know if I want another kid.' He finished me off.

'Well, maybe it was all for the best then.' I dropped it like a bomb. Then I cried from the guilt and shame and turned to wash the dishes.

Twenty-two pairs of sunglasses

That winter was a long string of shapeless days. Each morning I woke and saw the cold bay, a blanket of shadow and light that changed with the weather's mood and the repeating tide. In the early hours when I couldn't sleep, I would sip coffee and watch the tide turn, waiting for the sun to lift.

As the horizon began to burn orange, the water was grey but also not grey. Silver but also not silver. I could feel a memory slowly being drawn out. On the fifth day of watching, I remembered: my brother, about twelve, pulling thermometers to pieces at the desk in his bedroom. Us pushing the bubble of quicksilver – silver but not silver – around with our fingers. Even water has a memory.

By the time the sun had risen, the mercury bay was gone. It had turned a pale silver-blue. The trawlers headed out and the seagulls landed on the small slice of sand that pointed like a finger at the town opposite and formed the mouth of the creek. These noiseless flocks arrived one after the other until they reached quite a number. Then, as if keeping time, one after the other they left. By mid-morning they returned to tuck their heads under one wing and sleep just out of reach of the tide.

I had stepped out of my life and into someone else's. Into a house that locked from the inside but didn't have a key. At the front door a pair of medieval-looking bolts slid into place, securing the heavy double doors top and bottom. A short path led through an enclosed courtyard to a second door. From there I would enter, then lock the second door behind me. This was a design that kept the world out; it also made it hard to leave.

Once inside, the fortress-like entry gave way to air and light. A long room of glass faced towards the ocean and was wrapped by a deck that mimicked the bow of a boat. From inside this minimalist cube of glass it felt like I was floating above the water, about to take off. I lived here for two months, housesitting with my family, suspended above the tideline.

Not long after we moved in, a friend visited one morning. We stood in the living room and I showed her the view. When she was a child she lived in the village on the other side of the bay, she said. On weekends, she would bundle her pocket money up in handkerchiefs and tie them in a knot to her swimmers before swimming across the mouth of the creek to the town opposite with her friends. There they would buy lollies and play at the park. On special weekends, her father would row a small boat across so her family could go to the movie theatre. They would return home late at night. One time, the bioluminescence rolled brightly over her father's oars as he pulled them through the water towards home, she remembered. Another time, after watching *Jaws*, she stood resolutely on the jetty and refused to climb into the boat. Her father carried her.

This view always drew me to it. In the early mornings I watched the watery lines drawn slowly by the sun and moon. When I didn't watch the water, I noticed the clouds, rolling in heavy with the next storm or tracked loosely across the sky like a child's finger painting. It was a view where everything changed but nothing was different. I wondered if this was what it was like to talk with God.

I liked living with a horizon. The encouraging length of it all. As if the increased capacity for space – as far as the eye can see – also extended time.

A woman stands alone at a window and looks at the bay. She drinks coffee. She waits for the sun to come up.

On the first night I prepared dinner in the long white kitchen and realised there were no curtains to pull shut. Anyone could see inside, especially with the lights on. I felt exposed. As though we were on a movie set, unreal and unprotected, performing the rituals of a family dinner.

The mother sets the table. She calls the child and the husband to it. They sit down together and begin to eat.

This feeling of un-reality permeated throughout the next day. The house told me how to act. I cleaned compulsively. The beige furniture demanded it. I began to say 'don't' a lot.

'Don't eat on the lounge.'

'Don't wear your shoes inside.'

'Don't let the dog in.'

In an unexpected way, living in someone else's house meant stepping into a different set of rules. And it was easier at this point in my life to be someone else for a while. I understood this woman's wants and needs better than my own, largely because they fell in line with the demands of marriage and motherhood. Most importantly, I stayed on script.

The mother drops the child at day care. She returns home and cleans.

But things were not how they first seemed. The clutter-free minimalism hid a more private desire for things. In one drawer I found twenty-two pairs of women's sunglasses lined up in rows. Another was piled with crystal vases and delicate glass bowls. If I moved one, it became difficult to restore balance.

At home, I owned a single pair of sunglasses. I did not own any delicate glass bowls. My bowls were made of extra strong vitrelle and if I dropped them, they rarely broke. But occasionally, if it fell at just the right angle, the vitrelle would smash into a million pieces. In those protracted seconds between the bowl slipping and hitting the ground, I would wonder: will it bounce or shatter? In the short months before we moved into the glass house, I had felt like one of those bowls falling from the bench, unsure if I would bounce or explode. This can go on for years if you let it.

In the moment between falling and possibly bouncing, I chose to get serious about bedlinen. Before we started housesitting, I went out and dropped $300 on new sheets: glowing sateen cotton, white, 600 thread count. New pillowcases too. I made the bed perfectly each morning, turning down the top sheet into a straight line. Folding and tucking the end and sides snugly beneath the mattress so that whoever climbed in first that night would feel trapped.

But even with the beds made and the clothes put away, there was a moment each morning when, like clockwork, I suddenly felt as though I couldn't breathe. After breakfast and coffee and cartoons and getting dressed and getting my son dressed, an intense restlessness would settle in. It sat in my throat and on my chest. I would throw things into a bag in a terrible rush – if I didn't leave our house as soon as possible, I'd never get out.

The only way to dispel the suffocation was to throw the doors open and walk out onto the verandah. For a short time, I'd watch the birds – usually the magpies and delicate blue wrens – until everything else faded into the background and I could catch my breath.

In these moments I hardly recognised myself. I would bundle my son into the car as quickly as possible and get out of there. This is what I think people mean when they say *I just had to get out of the house*. Getting out of the house was easy now I had another house to go to.

Not long after we moved into the glass house, there was a storm. A night of rough winds turned the bay brown and foamy and shifted the sand opposite into new shapes. This made the mouth of the creek shallower, until just enough was left for the boats to pass. The seagulls had multiplied overnight, joined now by a dozen pelicans, who made the most of the shallows. They waded in and caught fish as they streamed out with the current. Did the birds glimpse the changed landscape from the sky, or did they know instinctively that a night of wind meant an easy breakfast the next day? Did the fish know what was coming?

Months earlier, towards the end of summer, I had walked past the wharf with its long timber boards and headed for the rocky shoreline. I saw a group of girls, laughing and screaming as clusters of children do, as they attempted to swim across the mouth of the creek to the beach opposite. The shallows on the other side caught all of them, except one, who found herself suddenly swept past the beach. She screamed, flailing madly while her friends banded together on the sand and watched, helpless. A woman, one of the girls' mothers, sprinted down the path past me, her face twisted by fear. I saw a man who'd been fishing from the rocky outcrop quickly remove his shoes and jump. Somehow, he made it to the girl. He dragged her out of the water and roughly onto the rocks, both gasping. A boat headed over to pick the stranded girls up from the beach. The locals aren't worried by these things. We know the current eases and you just catch a wave back to the beach.

These are the initiations of childhood. Testing our physical limits, often involving a body of water. Trials that usually teach us something important about ourselves if we're paying attention. When I was a little girl, I swam the same distance from one side to the other. At low tide, my brother and I dived off the wharf and headed for the beach opposite. Around half-way, at the deepest point where the current tugging my small body towards the bay became more insistent, I wasn't sure I would make it. Salt water stung my eyes and throat and my legs and arms burned. I could see my brother swimming ahead. Suddenly, I felt soft, sucking sand beneath my feet. I crawled onto the beach, legs shaking. I could see our mother waving from the jetty. I don't remember swimming back.

The mother stands on the jetty and worries if her child will make it to the beach.

What would happen if the mother jumped from the wharf? Would she make it to the beach on the other side? In a way what she does is harder. Letting go, watching, not saying 'don't'. It carries the recognition that we never really know our children, as Joan Didion wrote, partly because we can't see past our fear.

We don't know the mother either, standing on the wharf with one hand raised to block the sun from her eyes (someone should get her a pair of sunglasses). None of us can see past our idea of her. She wishes for the safe return of her child, of course, but what does she *want*? It almost sounds accusatory: *tell me what you want so I can know who you are.* Maybe she doesn't know herself.

I wouldn't know. Maybe a new pair of sunglasses. Could I be the type of woman who owns twenty-two pairs? If I had a moment to think, I might try to find something I wanted. I had wanted another baby, for a while. Part of the plan. When this became less and less likely, when he said *I don't want another kid* after miscarriage and another year of trying, I had to replace the plan with something else. Some other kind of wanting.

Except I had turned the wanting off to make room for children and I had become pretty good at it. I had already grieved the time and independence lost in that initial sharp adjustment to motherhood. I made my peace with it and was prepared for more of the same. I wasn't prepared for wanting.

On the many trips back and forth between home and coffee, either pushing Joey in the pram or sometimes carrying him when his legs grew tired, child on one hip and child's bike on the other, I window shopped. In one I saw a 'purpose' journal, designed for women who I imagined felt an acute erasure of self and desire. This journal sat alongside another notebook with *I am her* inscribed on the cover in elegant script, inviting those of us peering into shopfront windows to journal ourselves into existence. It seemed I wasn't the only woman who needed some encouragement. I could imagine the warm glow of journalling against the backdrop of the house. The beep beep beep of the washing machine, the pile of dirty dishes waiting in the sink, the lunches that needed to be planned for and packed.

The mother walks up and down the street pushing a small child in a pram.

There's an apathy at stake here. One that is an unspoken requirement for the debasement and self-annihilation of motherhood. An apathy of self. This is not the only option, but it remains a popular one. That was the pain in my chest. The knowledge that I didn't really matter any more. 'The conflict of familial life and creative identity,' Rachel Cusk calls it. You could remove the word 'creative' and just simply say, *the conflict of familial life and identity.* That I could watch the sun rise and feel simultaneously that I had never been born, and that I had never felt so painfully alive. Dissociation is its own kind of unreality.

Watching the waves curl into themselves from inside the glass house, I felt reassured. Those waves have rolled for aeons. I was a speck in their eternal rotation. I was nothing. What did I want to do with this short nothing?

I sat on the floor of the walk-in wardrobe and folded my son's clothes into neat piles while everything fell apart. After six weeks in the glass house my husband, who seemed to always know what he wanted, left. He would come back eventually; we weren't done with each other yet. But that night, after he left, I slept deeply for the first time in months.

Rabbit person

The rabbit, Eevee, is as still as a brown stone. Thump. A small tremor runs through the floor in warning. Thump; louder now. Telling the intruder (a smaller grey rabbit) he's on borrowed time. They both have their ears up and open like the smooth wide edges of a satellite. Every muscle is wound tight; Eevee is ready to fly.

It takes her a second to pin him to the ground and sink her two front teeth into his furred back. I pull her off him and the small rabbit flashes away under the bed. A grey cloud of fluff, light as thistledown, floats to the floor.

We name the little rabbit Blue, for this blue-grey fur the colour of a storm cloud. Eevee waits outside the door of the bedroom where he hides. Inside is the best patch of carpet in the house, cut into a warm square by the morning sun coming through the window. But the door will stay closed for a few more days. I'm in there making too much noise. I shouldn't be touching the small grey rabbit on his cheek where he likes it; this makes my fingers smell like him and Eevee's eyes widen at the betrayal. When I'm back on the lounge that night, she rubs the underside of her jaw along my foot to reclaim her territory. She licks my legs and ankles sweetly; brands my body as hers; scent a kind of ownership us humans live with but don't understand.

Until Blue begins to smell familiar. I leave the door of the room open and Eevee has her carpet back. She stretches out in the sun and lets him come a little closer. He buries his head against her body. He's just a baby, small and needy, half her size. She cleans his ears. *You are mine now*, she claims him. He becomes her shadow, his soft blue-grey body always a second behind. She eats and he follows. She shits and he follows. She intuits safety in his company. The familiar warm rabbit smells dragging up memories of tumbling around her mother's belly with her siblings, the hot tongue flicking along her ears and eyes. They take turns sleeping, one watching out for danger while the other closes their eyes briefly. Instinctively she tugs the fur from her dewlap in great mouthfuls and lines the inside of their plastic burrow with it. I relax a little and untuck my legs from underneath my body. I feel awake in a way I haven't in a long time.

Two months ago, there was a long dragging week where our dog Harley, a lanky Great Dane, became sick. The kilos fell off her until all you could see were her ribs sticking through her dull black coat. I took her to the vet. Cancer, everywhere.

'Once it gets to their lungs there's not much you can do,' the vet explained. I was told to go home and think about our options. The decision was made for us a few short days later. She leaned her giant body on my legs in the waiting room. Unable to stand on her own, her breathing coming in hard gasps. Every time another dog walked in, the slow heavy wag of her long tail hit the chair beside us in welcome.

'Do anything you can to help her, we just want a little more time,' I told the vet selfishly. Which came to nothing in the end. Her big head filled my lap and she left the world.

'My dog's dead,' Joey told a complete stranger at a café a few days later.

'Oh no, I'm sorry to hear that.'

'I'm getting a rabbit,' he continued.

At four years old, he was suddenly desperate for a rabbit. This wasn't a question because, apparently, I had promised him one a long time ago, with the caveat that we couldn't get a rabbit because Harley would probably kill it. With the subtlety of a sledgehammer – the bluntness of the very young – Harley was dead, so he could now get a rabbit. These two facts were inseparable to him.

I shrugged at the stranger. This wasn't as bad as the time he announced to a crowded table at a different café that his mum had a vagina. *Right there*. Pointing for emphasis.

I guess we're getting a rabbit.

When we pick Eevee up from the breeders, she is nine weeks old with oversized ears that stick straight up in the air. Her almond-shaped, deep brown eyes are lined in white. I bring her home in a small cardboard box. Here, Joey, something small to pour your love into. They sit quietly together on the lounge as he feeds her bits of carrot. The energy of the house changes overnight; our voices become lower and softer; our ears keener. We move more slowly and deliberately, so as not to scare the rabbit.

Over the next week, we watch as her curiosity begins to outweigh her fear. She ventures further each day, to smell our fingers and toes, sometimes lying just out of reach with her legs tucked tightly underneath her tiny, furred body.

Eevee soon knows about the fridge. She appears at our ankles out of nowhere every time it's opened and demands kale or spinach. Snatching the leaves with her teeth before disappearing under the dining table in triumph. Her nerves have now lost their edge and the wired rabbit energy of before finds a new outlet. She races on the rug in tight circles, jumps and twists in the air. The beating in her chest rising to a hum as the rushing heat of her blood takes over. Jump. A flop and roll exposing her soft white belly to the ceiling. We show our teeth and laugh.

In the middle of the night I hear Eevee hop slowly down the hallway. She stops outside our bedroom door and waits there a while. Her ears reach into our room, catching the small murmurs of sleep and the dry crackle of cotton sheets. It's a nocturnal soundscape she can read as our bodies, our breathing, reverberate off the walls and slip out under the door. She hears the shape of the dresser, the fly banging its head repeatedly against the window, a foot pushing back the sheet to get some air.

She makes sense of it: they're in the bed. Then she slow-hops back up the hallway without slipping. Her nails tap the acrylic boards. She does this several times through the night. I hear her coming. Clip clip clip. She's at the door again. Clip clip clip. She's back in the lounge room. If I let her in, she will sit at the end of the bed and keep watch all night. A tiny sentinel with poor short sight but excellent hearing. Nothing gets past those big ears.

When I was about ten years old, my oldest brother left suddenly and moved to Queensland. He was always kind to me – the big age difference between us didn't leave any room for the usual sibling battles. He would listen to my child's prattle and help me when I needed it, one time taking the training wheels off my bike and running alongside until I got the hang of it. I felt the jolt of loneliness at his departure. His absence like a change of season in our home. Something – someone I loved – suddenly missing. His room half emptied of his belongings as he left behind childish things and took only what he could carry.

On my birthday that year, he sent his best friend to our door in his place, who delivered into my arms a large stuffed pink rabbit. There's loneliness and then there's emptiness. Just like there's love and then there's the absence of love. Then there are rabbits.

Danny stirs beside me and rolls over. I close my eyes for a moment and start painting circles with my breath; in for four seconds, out for four seconds. Repeat. I can't switch off. My ears strain, listening out for her.

Clip clip clip.

Is she lonely?

One morning I sit on the floor with Eevee and tell her my secret: everyone feels so far away. I can see them talking but it's like I'm underwater. I can hear what they are saying, but I don't understand how the words fit together. I rub her cheek and her eyes close. Her fur like a child's blanket. This isn't how I wanted things to go. My hands shake and my mind jumps and stalls.

There's a knock: the gardener, Will, is here to help manage the bushland that is overwhelming the edges of our yard. For a second I want to run. I open the door.

'Hi! Come in. No, leave your shoes on. Please! Honestly, I need to wash the floors anyway. Can I make you a coffee?'

Humans, like rabbits, have a canny ability to hide their injuries. We call this high functioning. But I think Will, with his steady voice and bright blue eyes, can see right through me.

There's an orange glow to the living room and cartoons on the TV. Danny, Joey, and I sit alongside each other like marionettes forgotten on the shelf; feet tucked, heads resting to one side, legs outstretched. Joey doesn't stay still for long though, sitting first on one lap and then climbing onto the other. It's a room of screens and soft pillows. Elbows and knees. The rabbit has come to sense a pattern to these things and joins us after the sun sets. She buries herself against Danny, lengthening her body along his thigh. He scratches her cheek lightly and she closes her eyes for a moment. She begins to purr, the way rabbits do, by grinding her teeth together.

'Eevee, you're in my spot,' I joke. On our lounge there isn't enough room for all the things a husband and wife don't say to each other.

In the shopping centre car park, I reconcile the endlessness of time with the knowledge that life is finite. The way mothers do, grocery list in hand. Our existential reality persists in the eternal question: what's for dinner tonight, tomorrow night, the night after that? I only ever buy enough food for three days. Three is a good number: my son can count to three; there's three wishes and three little pigs; birth, marriage, death – a kind of triptych that hinges together and gives a human shape to things.

Besides, I can carry three days' worth of groceries into the house in one trip. Today there's still time to kill, so I get the groceries first, gliding the trolley along the smooth floors and staring into my phone. I have forgotten something; what? I try to operate somewhere beneath the fog. Then I leave the groceries warming in the car and go to my doctor's appointment.

I tell her the anxiety is back – that my anti-depressants ran out a month ago. That, in public, I feel a paranoia so intense I experience something like vertigo when people look at me. Worst at the shops; the sting of the fluorescent lights and the oppression of the crowd; the strain of keeping a smile; the small talk that revisits like a ghost late at night: Did I say that? Do they think I'm strange? Did they notice? Vertigo, like when you lean over the safety rail on the side of a cliff and forget, just for a second, your husband and child who need you, and imagine the liberation of falling into nothing. *I can't go on. I'll go on.*

I returned home and put my new medication on the highest shelf in the kitchen. It looked down on me like a small, rectangular god. I put all my hope into that cardboard box and swallowed my tablet every morning. After only a few days, I felt awake. I could see further and more clearly. I could bring my thoughts together and speak them out loud. I could say hello, hello to people as I walked by on the street, as you do in a small town, without wanting to disappear. I brought home a small blue-grey rabbit. Danny rolled his eyes. Joey was thrilled. Eevee stomped her foot in warning.

Women's time

It was the winter I gave up on gardening. Joey, then two years old, had started day care and discovered friends, and I receded a little more into the background, which is as it should be.

Suddenly I had time. Stretches that reminded me of school holidays stuck at home as a teenager. I'd flick the TV on and off; stand uselessly in front of the fridge, considering its contents; remove myself to the backyard; return to the TV. I thought a lot about having another baby. Somewhere within it all I quietly turned thirty-four.

I started going to the gym. There I found myself alongside women confident enough to wear crop tops in public. Some had their hair piled high on their heads in effortless mum-buns, topped with a bright scrunchie. I liked these women – they 'looked after themselves', in that put-together, Instagram way that I always struggled with.

These mothers weren't bored or tired, at least not on the surface. They drove big SUVs, ran their own businesses and, it seemed, had 2.5 children. Their nails were always done, their eyelashes filled, eyebrows tinted or dyed, perfect pairs of augmented breasts pushed up and proudly fake. I decided they were on to something. I bought a gold scrunchie.

Around this time, my hairdresser encouraged me to grow my fringe out – a commitment that takes months to achieve (I have failed before).

I signed myself up for the task and bought a pack of bobby pins. I pinned and sprayed the stray hair into place on top of my head, only for it to escape and fall in a useless heap over my eyes throughout the day. When it was successfully pinned back, I was left contemplating two imperfect dark brows.

I pencilled them in and felt ridiculous. My beautician tinted them, but still gaps appeared. No matter how hard I tried, they would not communicate the 'power brow' look I wanted, the look the women at the gym emulated. I considered spending $120 on a serum that guaranteed hair growth, but I'd already spent so much money in one lifetime trying to remove hair I couldn't justify the expense of now trying to regrow it.

'One of your eyebrows sits slightly higher than the other,' my beautician announced. It wasn't that they weren't symmetrical after all. The problem was the muscles on one side of my face were now weaker than the other side.

'A little bit of Botox would fix it,' she added.

I reconsidered my options. I cut my own fringe.

Then lockdown arrived and it was like Time had walked into my room and closed the door behind her.

There you are. She sighed, as if she had been looking for me for a while.

I didn't reply.

She sat on the end of my bed and made a minute feel like an eternity.

Stop it, I said.

I can't, she laughed.

Is time up? I asked.

It's never up.

Is it time?

No, it's 11:00 pm.

Some imagine Time as a man and a father. But Time is actually a woman, about middle age. I don't know if she has children, so I won't name her 'mother'. Somewhere deep inside her, there is a clock, its mainspring wound to the mechanism of her biology. I know this because I can hear it ticking.

I ignored her and got up. She followed me down the hall with my mother's voice.

You should get some sleep.

I turned the TV on. She fought me for the remote.

The ticking was so loud now it almost drowned her out.

GET SOME SLEEP OR YOU MIGHT REGRET IT, she yelled, holding the remote just out of reach.

Ironically, Time doesn't believe in regrets. She lived for the moment.

Life's too short. Live as if you were to die tomorrow. YOLO. These are her guideposts.

She started to stream *The Kardashians*.

We agreed that the interesting thing about this family is how much they change and yet stay completely the same. The way Botox can freeze a muscle, making it almost impossible for a woman to cry. We watched as Mother Kardashian slid into an MRI machine that looked like a smooth white egg. The doctors will tell her how old her body is – not the measurement of her birthdays, but her physiological age. She is pleased with the results.

'I'm forty!' she tells everyone. The same age as her second daughter, who is now rolling her eyes as her mother smiles into the camera. We all become our mothers, but few become their daughters.

The image of Mother Kardashian sliding from the egg reminded me of larvae hatching. One day time will catch up with her and she'll wrap herself in a cocoon of silk.

When I was a child, I kept silkworms under my bed in a shoebox and waited. I fed them mulberry leaves from the tree in our yard and was always impressed by their insatiable appetite. No matter how many leaves I crammed into their tiny cardboard home it was always empty the next morning. Their quiet chewing drifted up through my mattress at night and into my dreams. I dreamt of mulberry leaves and silk.

Each cocoon equals a mile of silk thread. I had to decide whether to boil them alive inside their cocoons and save the thread or let them break through. If allowed to hatch the thread would be broken in pieces but the cycle would continue. Each moth would lay as many eggs as possible to keep the species going and then die. This is how I learned the truth about silk manufacturing. Their cocoons are tiny woven coffins. I gave up on silk and waited for mine to hatch. When they cut through, I released their white powdery bodies next to the mulberry tree.

We were still watching *The Kardashians* when the world reopened. Beauty parlours revived overnight, and appointments stretched for months. I contacted a beautician in town, one I'd never been to before.

'I got you girl.' She fitted me in.

At our first appointment I explained the eyebrow problem and outlined my desire for something better than what I had; for evenness, balance. In eyebrows and, if I was being honest with myself, the rest of my body too.

'You don't need Botox,' her reassuring face floated upside-down above mine as she examined what she had to work with. I closed my eyes against the fluorescent light and drifted off into gossip and small talk. I told her how Joey was back at day care and work was picking up. That, in the meantime, I hoped for another baby. Because with more time on my hands during lockdowns, I had realised it was running out.

I walked into the massage parlour and told Time to stay in the waiting room, but she ignored me and followed me in. She watched as I removed my clothes and settled under the towel.

You've really let yourself go, she said.

Shut up.

'Tell me if you want softer or harder,' the masseuse whispered. She folded the towel draped over my body down until I was almost naked but not quite. Then she started wiping my body with a second towel.

As she worked, I listed the things I needed to do before I picked my son up: email this person, call that person, write that thing, confirm that other thing, double-check when that piece is due, pitch something – *anything*, finish off the marketing contract work that kept rolling on. Could I fit in a gym session? I needed a pen to write it all down, but I was pinned to the massage table by the tiny masseuse who stood on my back.

I made a mental note to get the shopping on the way home after school pick-up; do a load of laundry before dinner. What should I cook for dinner?

This is perhaps a woman's experience of time: its nihilistic anxiety; the biological ticking; the way it is filled easily with other people's needs; the creeping invisibility and the Botox. How it is measured by cycles and seasons that assert themselves rhythmically in the vestiges of blood and bodies – a temporality that has so little to do with linear time. A body like this makes itself felt.

'You are tight.' The masseuse rubbed the muscle that ran alongside my spine before moving back up to my shoulder. Down and up. Down and up. Things cracked and ground under the weight of her smooth forearm.

She sat behind me and pulled one of my arms behind my head, arching me backwards. My body stiffened.

She massaged the meaty part of my palm and pulled each of my fingers until they cracked.

She pinched my Achilles tendon and my eyes blinked involuntarily.

Her thumbs pressed under the arches of my uneven eyebrows and my ears popped.

'Try to relax.' She shook time from my body and for the rest of the hour I thought only of her warm hands.

The leather jacket, part 1

The jacket is age-worn and soft. Made of thick black leather with padded shoulders and brown piping edging the pockets. At its waist three buckles pull together, creating the quintessential eighties silhouette.

I found it hanging in the window of a vintage shop in Brighton, England. Down one of those quaint paved laneways, somewhere off Cranbourne Street, beneath coloured flags and flower boxes. I was there to deliver a conference paper at a symposium on contemporary women's writing, a PhD student eager to make a name for herself and waiting for her life to start. I didn't know it at the time, but I was free. Any responsibilities I had fell perfectly in line with what I wanted to do. I had just turned 28.

I'm still tethered to that woman, her dreams and her ambition, although she also frightens me. That I could ever be so single-minded, forgoing every other experience for one grand scheme. She was determined, this leather jacket woman – she had a five-year plan and was sticking to it! Admirably confident but also ashamedly opportunistic. The same woman who couldn't find time to visit her grandmother, who regularly missed her nieces' and nephews' birthday parties, who left and didn't look back.

She and I are, of course, one and the same, but we are also very different. It's not a bad thing, just life continuing in its casual way: accepting jobs that pay the bills, buying a house, starting a family.

I'm careful not to measure how things are now against that initial bloom of independence and ambition. Nothing would stand up in comparison. It's not a question of failure or success. There was a deeper shift that happened a few years into the five-year plan, when things were going well, and items were successfully being ticked off the list. Each time one goal post was reached, another took its place. This is the pattern of the overly ambitious.

I started to doubt whether it would result in any real success other than an unwavering ability to sacrifice everything else along the way. My determination faltered. Why was I doing this again? I realised I didn't want the same things any more. The jacket moved to the back of the wardrobe.

Years later, as I stand in front of my wardrobe overwhelmed by the amount of crap I have held onto, I don't know what to do with this bulky thing that I never wear. When England's cold seeped into my bones years earlier, the jacket had felt like a practical purchase and emulated the punk style of the young women I met in Brighton, with their shaved heads and vintage clothes. But here in Australia's sunshine, it always felt a little silly. A statement from another climate and a different time.

I let it fall heavily on the bed alongside the other clothes I've decided to give away because they no longer make the cut: tight black office dresses; shiny sequinned tops; a bright pair of pants I bought on a whim when I decided I wanted more colour in my wardrobe. These are the things I wanted at the time but now never wear.

Yet, despite its uselessness and how much space it takes up, at the last moment I return the leather jacket to the wardrobe. You could call it sentimental value. An oversized souvenir. It will always represent something else, a part of myself that I'm not willing to give up forever – that ambitious, motivated woman – even though it doesn't fit quite right.

Published in the *Guardian*, 2022

Part 2

Now I'm being haunted by this thing I wrote: *life continuing in its casual way*.

There's nothing casual about the decisions we make and why we make them. There's always momentum behind it, pushing us along. We give it names like capitalism, culture, patriarchy.

Can I be honest? I didn't have it in me, to keep working the way that I had at 28 – so single-mindedly – after I became a mother. Though I admire those who can, especially women who have unseen forces that pull, like gravity, at their clothes and ambitions. Let me put it simply: I felt my brain had changed after I had a baby. I changed. The whole world shifted on its axis. Warm was no longer warm enough. The sun was too bright. Night was day and vice versa. There was tummy time, and no time at all. It was complete torture; it was the best time of my life.

Before all that, back when I was a postgraduate, I became infatuated with a particular Irish-language poet. The translations of her poetry into English, the impenetrability of the originals in Irish, determined my research. After I left all that behind, I maintained a romantic view of motherhood, influenced by something I had read in this poet's essays; that after having her first child she overflowed with creativity and as a poet she was reborn. I was deeply attracted to the idea of motherhood as a creative wellspring and I never considered that the opposite could be true; that motherhood leaves less space and time for writing and, in some cases, the physiological effects of sleep deprivation and depression obstructs whatever desire is left. So, after the birth of my son, I waited patiently for the writing to flow.

Words left me. I couldn't concentrate. Or spell. I could barely read or write. At least, not the way I did before. I was humbled by what felt like failure.

After that experience, I became more interested in humility than success. Humility and care, which we've been told to avoid at all costs when, really, these aren't the problem; the problem is how these are so quickly devalued. A trick of the prejudicial eye that diminishes what has historically been cast as women's roles when care is the source of everything. Margaret Mead, an anthropologist, saw in the healed fragments of a thighbone evidence of civilisation's beginning. That for someone to break their leg, to then be carried and healed, loved, was where it all started. Without care, we wouldn't have survived.

I think about this as I sit on a wooden bench – Minnie Quinlan's bench – in Katoomba to email a friend. I'm away from my family. The first time I've travelled by myself since Joey was born, and I've already cried twice that morning at the distance between us. Against my back I can feel a brass plaque. The dedication to Minnie reads: 'who gave loving service to all'. It's the love that catches me.

Minnie arrived in Australia on her own at 22 in the 1880s, an assisted immigrant from Ireland via England. She was a domestic. Later, a volunteer for the local Red Cross. Town charlady; spinster; pensioner. Living on one pound a week in a house a local once described as a hovel. Towards the end of her life, she often sat in her favourite spot, a bench outside the post office, and chatted to the people who passed by. She died at 88; a disease of the heart.

And for her effort, a bench in her name where a stranger can rest a moment, seventy-four years later.

Minnie, were you equal parts strict and kind? I imagine you were. I imagine you poured extra milk in your tea. Took two sugars. That every night before falling asleep, you read secret romance novels that your friend Miss Ebbs, the librarian, slipped into your bag. Finding in these stories feelings that remind you of someone back in England before you boarded the awful SS *Abergeldie* – it makes you sick just thinking of it – to Australia.

I imagine that when you arrived, you found Sydney stifling, so you took to the mountains and settled here. You always liked the rain on the roof at night; the fog that drifted in silently to touch the windows; it reminded you of home. You sent letters encouraging your younger brother to make the same journey. You talked to strangers like they were family, the way people do when they are lonely.

Am I getting close to who you were, beyond the words on a plaque?

Humility is a bench dedicated to Minnie for her service to others. Minnie, who, I later read, gave more than she herself had. Which is incredibly sad and incredibly fraught – as women's unpaid labour and the financial vulnerability that accompanies it always is. But also, boundlessly generous.

How do we put ourselves at the centre of our own lives? How can we be humble and ambitious? How do we become more like Minnie and yet not end up like Minnie?

I'd have been a terrible charlady. To the disappointment of my mother and later my husband, I'm naturally untidy. But the words are coming back to me now; it just took some time. I can dust them off, tidy up the sentences. I can give loving service to language and ideas. Ambition is harder to return to because it has lost my trust. Still, I have post-ambition guilt. Because as a feminist, aren't I supposed to be driven and financially independent? As a woman – a mother and a wife now – aren't I supposed to put my family first? I try to be ambitious for the work and not myself. I think Minnie would understand.

Written at Varuna House, 2023

The death of Judy Plume

Late afternoon, just as the shade slides into the valley below, it's the fairy wren first. A nondescript brown. Hopping forward on its tiny, forked feet and impossibly thin legs, looking for something to eat on the deck.

Not that, not that. It lets out a frustrated shriek, the feathers on its head standing on end, its angry eye bright.

Next the grey fantail. Flopping in the air just off the verandah. How does it stay airborne as it twists impossibly for invisible bugs? It joins its partner in the gums nearby.

Now, the eastern spinebill that visits my kitchen window every morning. Hanging upside-down in the orange bottles of the banksia, getting drunk on nectar.

A magpie in the field below.

A kookaburra on the power lines.

A bird in the distance, too small to make out.

Another wren, following the path of the fairy wren moments before. It sees me and leaves.

I enter their names one by one into the app on my phone.

I'm thinking of the first day we saw our house. We had been looking for months and our list of desires were long, but I'll summarise: Danny wanted a garage, I wanted room for a chicken coop. We went out Saturday morning to stalk real estate agents, driving from Sanctuary Point to Basin View to Tomerong, following the zagging track of open houses.

The rain had washed out the road and I handled the car slowly down the hill, around potholes and the creviced paths made by the sudden unrelenting downpour of the night before.

Oh hell no. We were both thinking it. This is not *the one*.

Then we turned into the straight driveway and saw the cottage at the end. Colonial yellow with brown trim. Shrunk into the hill it sat on. I saw the early summer light spreading under the trees like crocheted sunshine. The chickens in the yard. How the birds were everywhere.

Danny saw the shed.

'Big,' he said as we climbed out of the car and met our fate.

We left saying no. *Not for us.* But the place had entered our minds and wouldn't leave. For a week all we could think of were the things we would do to it. We imagined a life that comes with a house like that. One of space and peace; idyllic and private. I laugh at us now. A house is a fantasy that sits alongside reality.

A week later, we stood in the yard and made an offer.

The cottage is small. There are two bedrooms at the end of a short hallway, a tiny bathroom, half a kitchen, and two fireplaces. At nearly one hundred years old it has not kept up with the storage demands of modern life and four years later the things we owned had outgrown the spaces we held for them. These things began to overflow: the children's Panadol shared a shelf with the cleaning products; above them, old craft projects Joey had completed, which I clung to like souvenirs from a past life. There was never enough room, and I was not the minimalist I'd fantasised.

I understand better now the lure of the suburban project home, with four bedrooms and a separate toilet. An entire room just for living. A kitchen with a walk-in pantry. No toys to step over (or on). Because no one had told me that space is the opposite of children.

The subject of selling came up.

Let's get a bigger house, less land. Let's sell and be happy. It was a new story we started to tell ourselves.

We began freshening the place up: painting, cleaning, gardening. Two weeks in, I got my nails done. Pointed acrylics painted gloss black. Long nails can complicate a great many daily tasks. I loved them for their impracticality, at a time when practicality meant so much. In hindsight, this may have been a subconscious rejection of the changes that were coming. I didn't want to be a sensible wife at home, doing the chores. I wanted to be fabulously useless. Deep down, I didn't want to move. Which brings me back to the birds, because I would miss them most of all.

The brown cuckoo doves.

The three lyrebirds that run across the driveway like tiny raptors.

The little finches with their red masks. How they play chicken with my car when I drive down the hill, darting out of the way at the last second.

There is a direction to these things – sell up, move out, settle down. Up, out, down – it reminded me of shovelling, which I had been doing a lot of, as I laid a new garden path and chipped my glossy nails. Metaphorical shovel in hand, we were digging our way out of debt while watching interest rates rise. We were lucky; we could buy an old house in the suburbs across the highway with the profits from selling an acreage that was desirable – what you pay these days for space and privacy. Our fantasy of adding a new kitchen to the cottage had been checked by the reality of building costs post-Covid. Selling now was the sensible thing to do. Still, hearts aren't known for common sense.

I visit a friend in her new home. After living in small studios or one-bedroom apartments with her husband and their child, the family now has space to spread out their lives. Only they don't.

'We follow each other from room to room,' she laughs. The lingering memory of how they've always lived since their daughter was born; on top of each other; in each other's faces; instilled in their bodies. After years of small quarters, they are unable to fill a larger home.

'She hasn't even played in her own room yet.' She gestures to her daughter, who carries her toys one by one into the lounge room where we sit and talk. The next time I visit, her daughter plays in her bedroom with Joey, and my friend is leaving her husband.

We live in the tension between reality and fantasy. Where homes and the bricks we build them with are more fragile than we think. I rewrite Three Little Pigs accordingly:

Blows down house of straw.

Blows down house of sticks.

Blows down house of bricks.

The wolf isn't real but his instinct to destroy is. The pigs aren't real either, but their instinct to build a structure around themselves, however flimsy, is familiar. It is a desire for home.

There's a word for this in Welsh: *hiraeth*. One of those untranslatables that are beautiful even as they slip between meaning to reveal, with an expansive absence, the shape of language. *Hiraeth* captures a feeling of home – of longing, nostalgia, wistfulness, and desire. It speaks of the loss of home that comes with colonisation and destruction of culture. The closest word we have in English is 'homesickness', but in that straightforward translation the subtleties are lost.

In the novel *Marrying Winterborne* by Lisa Kleypas, the character Rhys describes *hiraeth* as an unreachable destination of a kind: 'It's a longing for something that was lost, or never existed. You feel it for a person or a place, or a time in your life . . . it's a sadness of the soul. *Hiraeth* calls to a Welshman even when he's closest to happiness, reminding him that he's incomplete.'

It's a small, unhappy word; to be sad to one's soul, to feel incomplete, and to yearn so completely for a home that doesn't exist.

There are other words too. In German, *fernweh* is feeling homesick for a place you have never been to. In French, *dépaysement* is the feeling of being out of place and foreign. In Spanish, *querencia*, which confounds translators; on one hand it means a place from where you draw strength, but it is derived from the Spanish verb *querer*, which is closer to 'desire', and gently holds longing. *Querencia* is also the part of the bullring where the bull takes its stand.

And English, with its favour for the monosyllabic, leaves us without a word. The closest I can come up with is a deferred homecoming or un-arrival, a bittersweet home-sweet-home. A memory that is also a desire. Somewhere to make a last stand.

Once the garden path was laid, Danny and I turned to the shed, which housed boxes and two Commodores in various stages of decay and repair.

'There are boxes in here we've never unpacked,' he complained.

With Joey's help, I went through them one by one. Old pots and pans, some framed photographs.

Then one of the baby things I'd set aside that time I was pregnant for a few months. A box of everything I wouldn't have. Sometimes the fantasy isn't what we imagined.

I'm thinking of that time I raised chickens. And the death of Judy Plume.

When we moved into the cottage the previous inhabitants took the chickens but left the old coop. My friend Aimee, who has a brood of chickens, offered some newly hatched Wyandottes, the adults' plumage laced brown and black, and known to be good layers.

Judy Plume was one of four.

Judy Plume, Judy Garland, Judi Dench, and Sunday Roast (a rooster I didn't want) came to us at four weeks old, just as they were swapping fluff for spiny shafts that would soon be feathered. Judy Plume was the prettiest already, with golden highlights along the arches of her wings. I won't lie; I played favourites.

At night I kept the three Judys and Sunday Roast in a large box in my office to keep them warm. They were still babies after all. In the morning, I moved them to the chicken coop for a day of exercise and sunshine. Joey climbed through the tiny door of the coop each afternoon, scooped their frantic bodies into his arm and passed them to me one at a time so I could return them to their box in the office.

We kept this up for two weeks. Until I opened the door of my office one morning and walked into the plot of a Greek tragedy. The ill-fated Judy Plume lay limp on the bottom of the box, her feathers pulled from her body, while the other chickens – stained with their sister's blood – carried on their business, little half-feathered psychopaths devoid of empathy. It was my fault.

I called Aimee. 'Can you take the chickens back?'

The wolf blows down the chicken coop.

A few weeks after our cottage goes on the market we accept an offer. The sold sticker is applied and the fantasy is over; the chickens long gone, the fake nails removed. I see everything around me in this new light, which makes me notice what I've taken for granted. The old eucalyptus at the top of the driveway, standing like a queen's guard, a hollow between his knees; the tiny lizards that jump from under my feet when I come down the steps; the pink sky in late afternoon. And the birds. I write down their names so I will remember them.

Still, we all have a remarkable ability to reimagine these kinds of things. I start to build a new fantasy on Pinterest. I save images of timber floorboards, a big white kitchen, a desk in the spare room for writing. Espaliered fruit trees, skylights to bring the sun inside, exposed ceiling beams. I imagine family breakfasts every Sunday, Joey riding his pushbike down the street, a dishwasher. Danny wants a garage big enough for the Commodores.

This is how we begin to look for a new home, with the fantasy already in place. We wander through other people's houses and talk quietly about our possible lives there. We settle on a red-brick house and hope the wolf won't find us.

We can see the future

The party was somewhere in the bush.

'Where is it exactly?' I asked the host a week before, who is much younger than me and likes a party.

'Butt-fuck nowhere,' he replied.

That was entirely the point; to get high in the middle of nowhere. Nowhere a bridge to somewhere.

On the day, we leave the directions to Google Maps, which shows us the way until there's no internet connection and we have to trust the painted arrows nailed to the trees by the roadside are meant for us. After a long drive down unsealed roads, one arrow tells us to turn and our car slides into a clearing. We arrive just as the sun is setting. Six degrees out, our car warns. Doors slam. Calls of hello.

I carry in a gift and a plate of food, reminding myself of the older women who attended the dinner parties my mother hosted when I was a child, who always arrived with tin-foiled trays of appetisers and smelt of Chanel no. 5. The gift was appreciated, but unnecessary, our host said, wrapping his arms around me in a hug. The food was appreciated and devoured. An hour later a group of us sit around a fire ringed by stone, in cleared bushland between the mountain and the road in. The night is clear and cold. The Milky Way showing off in her purple dress.

Three young women split off from the group to dance under neon flashing lights. Bare arms waving, arses dropping to the earth, hips grinding. They take their pleasure without a second thought. There's nothing in front of them except their entire future, which can wait.

Not long after I turned 18, there was a long, sweating break between the HSC and the new year. My friends and I traded in the suburban heat of Narellan and took off down the coast to Wollongong. There was nothing in front of us except an entire future we could barely imagine and had imagined to death for the last twelve months. Army intakes, university open days, gap years, apprenticeships. Each of us had a plan we were only just beginning to set in motion. We baked on the sand and talked about the lives we didn't want: mostly, our parents' lives. Talking as if we were the first people in the world to cast off the expectations of family and mortgages. We planned our escape from the suburbs, as if our parents didn't do the same thing forty years earlier on a different beach.

'I'm never getting married and having kids,' I said.

At the party in the bush, I rotate like a pig on a spit: back to the fire, front to the fire. I like the slow-moving conversation of the sober and the slightly drunk in this circle. The easy laughs. The calm pace. But it's almost ten o'clock and I'm fading in the warmth of the fire. Usually, by this time, I would be in bed. Likely holding my son's small hand in my own while pretending to sleep. My knees begin to burn.

The night before, Danny had struggled to catch his breath and I drove him to Emergency. I waited in the hospital carpark for four hours with Joey asleep in his car seat. All clear. We returned home after midnight and fell straight into our cold beds. But Joey was restless, and I was called again and again to his side until all thoughts of sleep disappeared. I put my arms around my child and stared into the dark of his bedroom.

Long before the worries of husbands and late-night hospital visits, I moved into my first share house with three other girls. We partied on the edge of Ashfield next to the highway, dropping acid and watching the traffic lights stream red, green, and orange tails that softened the dark. I'd never seen anything more beautiful. I sat on the verandah under a heavy blanket until a housemate took me by the hand. She led me to her room, and I lay on her bed watching as she danced. She was life, her long skirt spinning out and catching her legs and hips. Her arms like ribbons. Spinning spinning. Her shadow followed and I hallucinated, without fear, that it was death one step behind. They danced together in perfect synchrony, a *pas de deux* of life and death. In the trance of her seduction, I fell asleep.

At the bush party, a few people disappear from the circle around the fire. The young girl in a tank top returns, pin-eyed and jittery, demanding the centre of the conversation, and the easy rolling banter of the group lags.

'Well, you're a fun bunch!' She shames us for our quiet. The circle breaks apart.

'I'm so fucking cold!' she exclaims. I look at her thin, bare shoulders and I want to tell her to put on a jacket. She storms back to dance under the neon lights with her friend following one step behind.

Danny stands with his mates to one side, holding a beer he's not drinking. After the anxiety and panic of the night before he doesn't want to lose control, but he still feels the need to perform. I wander over and hover silently at his elbow. A quiet wife-shadow, a common sight at parties. The three of them are talking about the dynamics of dating single mums, which is a new situation for one of the men.

'If ya just there for pussy, that's wrong mate,' one slurs to him. 'She's got a kid. Ya need to show her respect, mate.'

Danny and I listen.

'Yeah, brother. I do.'

'Cause the kid needs to see that or it'll fuck 'em up. Ya know?'

'I'm ready to go,' I whisper to Danny.

'It's only early. Let's stay a bit longer.'

'Okay, but soon.'

When I turn thirty-six, I throw a party. Twenty people gather around long tables we push together on the verandah. We line up empty wine bottles down the centre and stuff them with tall taper candles, but the wind picks up and they sputter out. We serve spaghetti bolognese and dirty martinis in small delicate glasses. Quiet wives and girlfriends sit beside their partners. I've always liked talking with the quiet women sitting at tables. We match each other's energy. They are often funny. I sit and listen, without the pressure of entertaining, safe in the company of good people. Sometimes we talk of our children and how they take our breath away, recounting the things they say that make us laugh. How they surprise us with truths we can't refute but have, somewhere on the way to adulthood, learned to live with.

My son is sleeping over at his grandma's house tonight, so I let loose for the first time in years. I throw back cocktails and champagne. I roll a joint and hand it to a friend who I know enjoys this guilty pleasure on occasion. He hands it back to me.

'I need to be home in an hour for the kids,' he explains.

I store it in my bra for later. I get into a conversation about children with a friend who has decided not to have any. He is younger than me by about ten years.

'I think having children is a selfish thing to do.' He surprises me with his truth.

I was taught the opposite, that not having children was a selfish thing to do. We look at each other from a great distance, a deep valley between us, each side formed by the shifting definitions of selfishness we had learnt throughout our lives. Both of us selfish in our own way. I remember the joint hiding in my bra for later, offering me a bridge.

By the time later rolls around, it's 3 am. Everyone has gone home except for six of us who sit around the fire pit, my husband and another man talking quietly to one side, and three other women – all older than me by about ten years. Women who know themselves beyond the shape of ex-husbands and ex-wives. It's not by chance that I'm here with them. Those my age have already driven home and returned to their young children. Usually I would do the same. Instead, I fish out what's left of the joint and refuse to share it with anyone. We cackle and drink and smoke, eyeliner and mascara running. Incongruent, midnight hags. All we need is a cauldron and the beginning of a Shakespeare play. We can see the future.

Why I love my chainsaw

When spring arrived we stood in the yard and surveyed the neglected garden. The trees around the house were taking over; saplings doubling their numbers and branches risked falling onto powerlines. The lawn was long, neglected for weeks, and full of weeds. We busied ourselves around the house. Danny mowed the lawn and sprayed the bindi. Joey organised his dinosaurs in a row and dug in his sandpit. I started to clean.

Like most housework, cleaning can go on and on once you get into the swing of it. I cleaned the bathroom, then the laundry. I washed the dog and her bed. I decided to tidy the verandah and went for the leaf blower hidden at the back of the shed. I couldn't get it started.

'I'm getting rid of this piece of shit!' I threatened. Danny laughed.

Back when I first wanted a leaf blower, I showed Danny an electric one online.

'We should get a petrol one,' he said confidently.

I acquiesced, the way Mum would when Dad decided things for the two of them, only to complain later when it wasn't what she wanted. I don't know much about blowers – electric or otherwise – except that

I had seen the one my aunty used to blow the dust and leaves from her wide country verandah with the press of a button. It was a housework revelation. I wanted the same.

The one we came home with was not the same. It was larger and bulkier. To start the small motor, you had to yank on a cord, which I soon learned is more difficult than it looks, demanding a mix of strength and coordination – hold it *down* while pulling the cord *up*, fast. It requires petrol mixed carefully with oil in a ratio I can never remember. There were three different buttons that all did something. It filled me with self-doubt; incompetence that led to a pitiable female helplessness inspired by the company of engines and oil. That day Danny started it for me and off I went.

A week later, he was at work, and I couldn't get the damn thing going. I wrestled furiously with the cord. I double-checked the petrol. I pressed all the buttons. I gave up and bought a broom. The blower sat uselessly in the garden shed for a long time. Every time I needed it, I would complain to Danny and remind him of the electric one. Its small, lightweight body possible because of the lithium-ion battery that sits at its core.

Around this time, my dad went downhill, and he went to hospital for several weeks. Mum was thrown suddenly into a pseudo-single life. She called, frustrated by her own lawn; she couldn't start the mower. I recognised it immediately, this helplessness, only this time it was coloured by grief. Without Dad, their careful dance of 'his and her' housework was out of step. The result of a lifetime of intimacy and interdependence that finds its shape in relationships between men and women, perhaps even between men and men, and women and women. I didn't know any better.

So, when Danny offered to start the blower this time, I refused. I carefully mixed the oil and petrol, I pulled the cord like I knew what I was doing, and it roared to life. I still hated it.

Once there was nothing left to clean outside, I surveyed the yard again. Inside the fence line – our backyard closest to the house — it was neat. Reaching a controlled suburban perfection that's difficult in the bush. But that's only about 5 per cent of the property. The rest was a tangle of pittosporum, bracken and native raspberry under a canopy of white gums and turpentines, the kind of acreage that demands power tools and weeks of fire prep each year. Again, I saw the branches closing in around the house and saplings of wattle shooting up.

When I showed Danny a small battery-operated chainsaw online that night, he was adamant.

'We should get a petrol one,' he said confidently.

I put my foot down and it stayed there for the better part of an hour. The next day he came home with my electric chainsaw. Its metal and plastic body is small and light, its chain not intimidating. I spent the rest of the week delightfully independent, cutting branches and chopping kindling in thick rubber boots.

This is why I love my chainsaw. It's something my mother would never use, and my dad would never have bought in his youth (although he borrows it all the time now). It doesn't need petrol or oil. Just a battery and a power point, which I understand. I also wasn't convinced – despite Danny's efforts – to give it up and buy something else that I didn't really want and probably would never use. I have no complaints; my chainsaw is perfect.

Danny returned home from Bunnings with a battery-operated blower for work. He's thrilled.

Michelangelo

The ceramic juicer was light blue. I had no intention of buying it, I just wanted to hold it for a moment; to enjoy the weight of it and admire its milky glaze. It was handmade, the kind of juicer that required an orange halved. Twist twist and in a minute, you had juice. Never enough to fill a glass, but that didn't matter. When I was a child it was the spinning dance that I had liked, when Dad would stand at the kitchen bench on a Sunday morning and I'd watch him juice several oranges by hand until he accomplished a small cup.

I turned it over in my hand and examined the small sticker on its base. $30.

'Don't get that, you'll never use it and it's too expensive,' Mum whispered over my shoulder. I immediately bought it. The stallholder, the woman who had made the blue juicer and several others, carefully wrapped it in brown paper. I slipped it into my bag.

Whenever I use the juicer, often for my own child, I feel an intense pleasure; the rebellion tied to my mother's disapproval.

Do other thirty-five-year-olds get off on doing the things their mothers tell them not to do?

I was raised in a strict home with rules I didn't agree with but obeyed anyway, because I was just a kid and easily punished. Rules I felt were always defined by gender. Like household chores – dishes, washing the clothes – while my brothers got to use the ride-on mower or build things with Dad. There were things boys did, and there were things girls did; boys could have motorbikes and do the whipper snipping; girls could polish the furniture and hang the washing out. Boys could go out late, girls stayed at home. On the other hand, girls could wear earrings (not too many, that made you 'common') and boys could not. I remember my brother, his eyebrow newly pierced and bright red, exiled on the verandah and not allowed inside the house until he removed it. The message was clear: our bodies were not our own. Boy or girl, none of us were allowed to get a tattoo.

The tattooist, Tito, is an artist and a surfer. When he isn't working, he's in the ocean alongside the other surfers down at Golfy Reef. He shows me two tattoo designs he's drawn in response to my booking request. I pick the simplest and sit nervously in the waiting room. The studio is well lit, clean, and white; a far cry from the bikie-run parlours when I grew up, with their dirty windows and always someone outside straddling a motorbike. Here, there was art on every wall. Opposite, two halves of a broken skateboard have been reassembled in the shape of a heart, hung alongside drawings of tigers and roses, while Kermit the frog stared at me from another frame.

Tito, who seemed to be always smiling, asks where I would like the tattoo. We decide on the territory: lower left bicep.

'Let's do it,' he smiles again, and I lie down on the black vinyl bed.

The ink enters quickly.

'Okay?'

'It hurts less than I thought it would,' I smile back.

On the wall above me is a large tapestry, deep red with gold tassels on its edges and images of cherubs tumbling playfully, like Michelangelo's Sistine chapel. At its centre sit giant dominoes in the shape of a

87

crucifix – a twisted renaissance. The barbed wire cascading from the top gives it a sinister vibe.

'I like the tapestry,' I gesture up with my eyes.

'Ahhh yeah,' Tito says in his slow Caribbean surfer-drawl. 'That was made by the local Van Gogh.'

'Oh?'

'Yeah really. He cut his own thumbs off.'

Tito's left thumb keeps my skin in place while the tattoo needle moves rapidly. His other thumb anchors the vibrating gun.

'It would have been hard to do the barbed wire without thumbs,' he adds. He wipes down his work with Vaseline and examines it closely.

I'm shocked into quiet. I imagine the pain of cutting through skin and nerve and bone. In Ancient Rome some men removed their thumbs to avoid conscription. Without their thumbs, they could no longer wield a sword. But if they were caught, the price was high. Some men were stripped of their titles and money, or if from a lower class, sentenced to death.

'How are you feeling?' Tito asks.

My fingers, I realise, are completely numb under the pressure of his forearm that pins my arm down. I wiggle them.

'I'm okay.'

We had been at it for almost an hour, and I was surprised by how much I was enjoying myself. The dig dig dig of ink and needle as it entered under my skin was relaxing.

'It's kind of meditative,' I say. There's nothing to do but wait.

Tito carefully mixes red and yellow until he achieves a bright orange.

'How's this colour for the mask?'

'Perfect.'

The hardest thing about tattooing is knowing how long it will take, Tito reveals. Some of his customers describe a tattoo as 'small', but it ends up being big, or vice versa. Once a customer asked for a row of skulls thirty-five centimetres long. He took the booking but ignored the measurement, thinking it was a typo in the booking form. It wasn't.

'It was huge, wrapping all the way around her leg, and took most of the day,' he laughs.

I look up at the twisted rug again.

Why remove your thumbs? I imagine asking Van Gogh.

Probably the same reason he makes art. Maybe it's not our thumbs that make us human but the way we choose to use them. Or the terrible desire to remove them, tearing, from our bodies.

My tattoo was finished. In the mirror it was my arm and not my arm. A small ninja-turtle – my own Michelangelo – smiled back at me in his orange mask. When I was little, I would dress up in my brother's ninja-turtle costume and become something else. Something that sat outside the rules.

Tito covers it in a thin translucent plastic called 'second skin'. I will be allowed to shed this second skin in a week. I run my finger over the black lines, feeling the slight rise of the ink just below the skin. It feels hot, like an injury or infection, which I suppose it is.

'You can use Bepanthen to help it heal,' Tito says.

'I have plenty of that.'

'The mothers always do,' he laughs.

Middle-life

In late autumn, I often escape the cool shade of our rainforested home and find the sun at the closest beach. I start my walk on the concrete path that runs above the shoreline but always, eventually, I'm called to the sand like a child. I remove my shoes and socks and place them at the foot of the stairs. This is how a walk, with all its promises of vigour, becomes a dawdle. Which is much better.

This morning I arrived too late to join with the early walkers, who release their dogs to the tide. But I'm not alone. A young couple huddle on a wooden bench near the stairs, kissing. Taking a private moment on an empty beach. I pretend I don't see them, looking instead out over the water. Past the headlands that stop the swells coming in from the Tasman Sea. From those headlands, on a clear day, you can see whales in their slow migration north.

The romantic in me knows this bay by heart. Its slow steady rhythms were the accompaniment for every weekend I can remember as a child, when my family would leave south-west Sydney on a Friday afternoon and head for our blue fibro shack down here by the creek. Those weekends were quiet and solitary, in a town where I didn't know anyone my age, and so I would walk (dawdle) up and down the beach, often finishing a book in a day. At night I'd lie awake beneath heavy woollen blankets and listen to the waves, hoping for the thrill of a lightning storm to flash between the thin aluminium shutters. After a storm, I'd wake to find the sands at the mouth of the creek had been moved in great handfuls, as if by giants, revealing wave-cut rock with furrows and channels like the lines of a board game that made sense only when viewed from above. I knew it as a giant's landscape, mythic and changeable with the tide.

I remember the weekend Dad bought a metal detector at a garage sale around the corner. He threw coins into the garden beds and instructed my brother and me to find them. Bored, I soon drifted off somewhere. But my brother caught on quickly, spending the rest of the weekend digging and digging, searching the beach for lost things. He returned at the end of that day with a rusted can, a broken chain and other lost treasures.

Now, the blue fibro shack down by the creek is long gone, replaced by the new owners with two brick townhouses. Only the beach from my childhood is still here; the sand holding a great number of lost things. At the end of the beach I find a smooth rock and reach for it. I send it out across the water.

I say I know this bay by heart, but really, I only know the shoreline that curves along the north. I haven't visited the old lighthouse on the headlands opposite since childhood. I don't know the depths of the bay, or the sandstone cliffs, or the sea caves. I only recognise its wildness from a distance and keep to the shallows, along with the other mothers and their children.

But when I am instructed to close my eyes and imagine a place where I feel safe, it's here. Waist-deep in autumn under a big sky. This is the same beach I walked with my boyfriend when, at twenty-one, I realised it was love. The same beach we returned to for our honeymoon five years later, staying a week in the blue fibro shack. I can't remember what we spoke of then, but I imagine it went like this:

'Here, try this one.' *I love you.*

'Four skips!' *I love you too.*

A kiss followed by a swim.

Now, like then, my eyes search for flat stones brought to shore by the tide. Weighing them expertly in the palm of my hand, I send them out again to skip across the surface of the ocean.

A year after we fell in love, I gave him a thick silver ring. Inside I had the jeweller engrave a memory: *skimming stones in Huskisson.*

It's been fifteen years. A marriage that was also a growing-up together. While I still dawdle, Danny strides ahead with intention. I slowly follow, along beaches, through shopping centres or carparks, down streets and pathways. He often arrives at our destination first and stands there, arms folded, wearing his impatience like a mask. I reach for him and we go in together.

My husband is not old; he is not young any more either. Neither am I. We are in this strange middle-life. He calls this *our years for working* and I try to follow his lead. Somewhere in the oscillation of work and family, though, I feel something has been lost. Maybe it is that girl wandering the beach, looking for rocks and hoping for a storm. In recent months I've become aware of how complicit I have been in my own disappearance. More wife and mother than myself. My body feeling strangely like someone else's.

The perfect stone for skimming must be light and smooth. Its curve needs to fit in the crook between forefinger and thumb. Most often, these are the thin black stones shaped like small surfboards, oval and smooth from the caress of sand and water. Once you find the right stone, it's all in the wrist. I can get up to five skips on a good day. Not a world record by any means, but enough to beat my husband regularly. Which makes me the stone-skipping champion in our family and prickles, delightfully, his competitive bone.

Our love felt inevitable. I passed him in the hall at school and thought he was cute. He sat behind me in maths and thought I was cute, but we never spoke to each other. Later, when we were twenty and ran into each other at the pub, we weren't weighed down by any sad history or high school memories fuelled by high-octane teenage love that eventually burns out – another kind of inevitable. We knew each other, the way you know the people you grow up alongside, but we were also strangers. Late at night, after we finished our shifts at the shopping centre where we both worked, him in his Woollies uniform and me in my best receptionist clothes, we would kiss in the empty carpark. He'd whisper Skid Row lyrics and we'd call it poetry.

Recently, when I became a stranger and we couldn't stand being in the same room as each other, it could easily have ended. And yet it didn't.

And yet. I think about that now. That the distance between together and apart lies in a conjunction. That a marriage stands on sand. That it is vulnerable to movement and there will be storms – there have been. Still, I like to believe that underneath it all, formed by all the changes and the years, there is rock.

We found our way back to each other in the silences. In his quiet looks: the way, almost imperceptibly, he bites the inside of his cheek when he becomes nervous; in the moment before he says 'I love you', when I can see it in his body and feel it in his hands, recognising the thought turning over in his mind before he speaks.

I love you.

Say it back or it floats away.

I love you, too.

Who is I? Where are you?

To say it is to shore ourselves up against another. Using his body as a cartographer's map, I lost my own. Now I understand that to love someone is to risk everything.

'Choose someone who loves you more than you love them,' a friend, married and drunk, once advised me. I wasn't sure if he said this because he felt the risk was too much or because, deep down, he feared he was unlovable. I thought immediately of his wife. How painful, to be the one doing all the loving.

A few weeks ago, my husband started sleeping on the couch every night because our bed makes his bad shoulder ache. I tried not to take this personally and believed him when he says it's his shoulder and not some other unspoken thing between us. I've missed his heavy shape beside me at night. His legs warming my cold feet. His lips and sighs. Our sleeping hearts meeting somewhere beneath the blankets. I've traded him for the small shape of our child who kicks, and the smaller lump of our dog who sighs in her sleep at the foot of the bed.

At a party a friend talks about a deep love.

'Do you mean chemistry?' I ask. Thinking of another friend's comment earlier in the week that chemistry can mean great sex, but not necessarily a good relationship.

'Not chemistry. This is when you're with your lover and it's like they are themselves and they are also you. You're the same person, but you're also different people. Like you can see yourself in them.' Her eyes are locked on her partner in recognition. Soulmates.

Another couple nod and lean towards one another. There's no space between them.

Like Catherine and Heathcliff. *'He's more myself than I am. Whatever our souls are made of, his and mine are the same.'*

Eternity in two bodies.

Danny wanders over.

'What are you talking about?'

'Soulmates,' I whisper.

'Oh,' he replies, 'I can't wait to meet mine.'

We both laugh, breathless. His sarcasm always delivering this familiar jolt that feels like us.

Soul – another word for breath.

Is it his soul that keeps me in place? When I don't know myself, he reminds me. I run my finger down the length of his spine and wonder at the distance between us. After fifteen years, where does he begin and where do I end? My finger like a bridge above a river. Saltlines, heartlines. The lines that tie us to each other, that bind our ankles and our wrists, hands cupped in offering and acceptance. Get on your knees; a sweet annihilation. I kiss the salt from his shoulder and he sighs. Kissing him is like swimming in the ocean.

My husband returns one night to our bed with an extra pillow for his bad shoulder. My body is suddenly caught between two opposing desires: my son, who wishes to remain each night beside me and Danny, who insists it can't be so. If they aren't careful, they will tear me in two. I choose my husband, and in this way, I fail my son. The way mothers with their own desires always fail their children.

At the beach the wind begins to lift the waves. Dragging the sand and leaving behind heavier things. The water reaches my feet and freezes them there.

Shark

I wake early and leave home in the dark. Drive past the resolute women who run the streets at this hour in activewear and smart watches. It might be the only chance they have, even on a Saturday, to do this thing for themselves. To put one foot in front of the other, and then the other, to swing their arms freely under an early dawn sky, until their inevitable turn towards home and whatever waits for them there. Sleepy children, eggs for breakfast. Maybe a man warming their bed.

By the time I get to the boat ramp, the sun has found the horizon. Dylan, our skipper for the day, stands in the middle of his boat in hoodie and crocs, welcoming the bleary-eyed travellers aboard.

'How are you feeling?' he calls to me.

'A bit nervous.'

'You'll be fine!'

I step off the solid timber jetty and feel the boat sag underneath me.

Sad middle-aged woman takes to the sea. I keep this thought to myself.

As we wait for the others, I talk with a man from Bateman's Bay. He has his own orange flippers, weight belt, and snorkel. Like me, he's here by himself.

Dylan offers us sea-sickness tablets and I take two. Four more people arrive; a couple who sit close to each other on the cold metal seats, and two friends who could be sisters.

We pull away from land and slide past the sail boats anchored in the creek: *Moonshine, Grace, Steel Away*. Other boats are named for their refinement or turned into jokes. This is a modern phenomenon, different to how seaworthy vessels were traditionally and superstitiously named after deities or spirits to encourage a sailor's protection at sea. These days the most popular names for boats are *Liberty* and *Escape*. Is that what people hope to find out there?

'Grey Nurse Sharks were hunted ruthlessly in the fifties – almost to extinction,' Dylan explains over the hum of the engine behind our backs, reminding us why we're here.

'They were the first shark to go in protection in 1992 and belong to the same family as the Great White. They sleep most of the day, shutting down half their brain and just cruising around.'

'Sharks are the ultimate predator. Every part of them is designed for hunting in the water,' he adds.

Then he assures us we will be perfectly safe freediving alongside them.

As far as swimming with sharks goes, Grey Nurse Sharks are at the easy end. Brodie, a twenty-one-year-old underwater photographer with thick silver rings and bare feet, has done this dive before. He's just booked a trip to Tiger Island in the Maldives later in the year, where he'll learn to swim with Tiger Sharks. 'They teach you how to spin them and push them away when they approach you,' he explains.

'Aren't you scared?'

'No, I'm just interested. If you enter the water with respect and want to learn, it's different,' he shrugs. He doesn't seem like the type to feel afraid.

We're out of the creek and start to pick up speed, heading east with the sun in our eyes. Under the wind and hum of the engine we all fall silent. In the quiet, I try not to think about the events of the last week. How my husband had moved out and wasn't coming back. But I keep thinking of him. I push the thought away and it bounces back up. I'm not crying. It's just water droplets flicking from the boat's canopy after a cold night as we cut along the flat surface of the bay. I moved past tears days ago, to the act that lies beyond that. A kind of soundless sobbing that twists inside your chest and stretches down into your guts. Like a sickness you try to expel. Maybe this is how the body ejects something that used to be love.

Or maybe I was expelling a small ugly fear I've carried inside for a long time: that I'll waste my life trying to make the man I love happy, when he hasn't wanted me for a long time. Throughout the long painful months when my marriage was ending, I often asked myself what I could do to fix it. The question I never asked was more important: what am I most afraid of, wasting my life or starting again? I belt my arms around me to stop myself flying loose.

At the mouth of the bay, we pass three small fishing boats. Our boat hugs the coastline as we make our way around the immense headlands and spy into sea caves about 30 kilometres from the edge of the continental shelf. I stare up at the towering vertical cliffs that look like the pages of stacked books. Layered and shaped over millennia. Timeless ancient stone.

'Sharks have been on this planet for over 400 million years, which is longer than trees,' says Dylan. 'But we kill about 80 million sharks every year. The problem is, if you remove the apex predators from the environment you end up with dead zones. What I think we need to do is learn to live alongside of them.'

How do you live with fear?

I watch as each wave lands against the base of the flat cliffs and retreats. The water left behind runs down slowly like a lover's hand. The couple sitting in front of me draw closer together and share it all, pointing and whispering.

We dip and rise on the threaded ocean, above currents that write love notes on the water to each other. Everything is soft and moving, a system of forces pushing and giving way.

Dylan calls being in nature therapy.

'I discovered the meaning of life on a mushroom trip,' he laughs. He couldn't remember what that meaning was the next day, but it changed him. He quit concreting to focus on diving and became a passionate environmentalist. He and his partner Lara bought a boat and started their own freediving business five years ago, becoming vocal advocates for the marine park our small village sits alongside. It hasn't been easy for them.

Three years ago, fishermen competing in an annual tournament that encouraged shark fishing caught two Tiger Sharks. As these sharks were weighed on Huskisson wharf a passer-by filmed the catch and sent it to Lara and Dylan. The couple shared the video on their social media in outrage that these tournaments still occur in the bay, targeting big game including sharks even though some species are classified as endangered or threatened.

'All the local businesses here rely on tourism, and that tourism depends on the health of the marine park. I just didn't think it reflected our values and the values of the community,' Lara said.

When they returned at the end of the day, they passed the fishing boats tied at Huskisson Wharf and felt everyone's eyes on them. 'Something just didn't feel right,' Dylan said.

'Even our customers picked up on it,' added Lara.

When they arrived back at Woollamia Boat Ramp it was deserted. Their signage had been vandalised and one decapitated Tiger Shark head had been left on the bonnet of their car.

'It was horrible. We were on edge for months after. Always looking over our shoulder. We have to work out of Woollamia Boat Ramp and they have their fishing club there. We were constantly death stared at. Some of our customers and parents who had our business stickers on their car were verbally abused.'

The video of the dead Tiger Sharks they shared on social media went viral. Thousands of people commented and shared it. Petitions were started. Tournament sponsors were called repeatedly. The backlash on Dylan and Lara was intense but so was the overwhelming support. Within a few weeks, the tournament announced all big game will now be catch and release. I'm not sure release is any less painful. Neither do Dylan and Lara, who call it torture. To be hooked, trailed along, left hanging.

We spot a man fishing from one of the cliffs. He has abseiled down the expanse and stands, feet apart, above us. A bright orange float vibrates wildly on the line as he fights something beneath the water. Suddenly, a silver fish is pulled from the sea.

Dylan brings us closer to the shore and we drift under a small waterfall that casts double rainbows above our heads. He holds us here at the mouth of another sea cave for a short while as we take photos and videos. Then we keep going. We're heading for The Drum and Drumsticks – a rock formation that resembles its namesake from the air. Up until the 1980s the area had been used for target practice by the navy. It's also an important cultural site of the Jerrinja and Wandi Wandian people.

'There they are,' Dylan says, pointing at nothing. It takes a moment for my eyes to find the brown seals on the brown rocks, where they bark and drag their immense bodies. 'Time to get your wetsuits on.'

We each struggle into damp suits that wrap around our neck and over our heads. Before we assemble on the stern, Dylan reminds us not to touch the seals.

'They have the jaw strength of a small bear so they could rip your arm off.' He says everything with a laugh, in the light-hearted way that is common with saltwater people. With that, we drop into the ocean one by one.

I float face-down on the surface in goggles and snorkel. This isn't a beach or a pool. It is a wild place. The neoprene is tight over my ears and all I can hear is the bone-echo of my breath moving fast through the plastic snorkel. I try to breathe more slowly and move my long flippers to keep up with the group. My eyes swing left to right. All I can see are bubbles. Streams of bubbles, like a gymnast's ribbon twisting. I reach out and feel the rising air go around and over my hand. The bubbles are colder than the water. Suddenly the seals are in front of me.

There are dozens and dozens, their big bodies spinning easily in the water. One glides below me and I'm caught in the creature's big round eye. They are curious and want to swim with us. The smaller ones move sharp and quick, like they have something to prove. They blow big bubbles in warning. This is their territory. The humans begin to plunge and spin alongside them. An hour turns to minutes. Too soon, we head back to the boat and the pack of seals follow us, like a friend farewelling you at the door.

Back on the boat we drink hot chocolate and eat Lara's homemade banana bread. There's a storm rolling in and the sky ahead is grey and dark. We turn into it and towards the Grey Nurse Sharks sliding oblivious on the bottom of the ocean near Bowen Island. They like to keep to the shallows. Preferring the rock shelves and reefs closest to the shore. This is what makes them susceptible to line fishing, Dylan explains.

'You will probably see some trailing lines or injured with hooks,' he says. We talk about the misconceptions people have about sharks as man-hunting predators and our instinct to run (swim) away. 'When you meet a shark, you shouldn't swim away. You need to turn and face it. Lengthen your body so they can see your size. Look them in the eye and make yourself tall,' Dylan says. I don't feel tall.

Loving you just doesn't feel natural, my husband had said. *I don't even know if I do any more.*

The only reason I'm with you is because we have a kid.

Again, we line up and drop one by one into the ocean. I surprise myself by being the first in the water.

A group of sharks can be called a herd, a frenzy, or a shiver. I like the last best. A shiver of sharks. The sight of them sends that tremble up my spine. There are too many to count. They move slowly in lines and slow curves. Some are 3 metres long, with large pointed dorsal fins and slitted gills. One just a pup, stuck to its mother's side as they move in familial synchronicity.

Sharks have electromagnetic sensors that can detect a heartbeat under water. Like intuition, they feel us nearby before we even see them. I would like to have this ability. To sense what is coming. It could stop a person from being blindsided. Then again, maybe it's best to stay in the dark as long as possible and pretend everything is normal. But the fear is still there even if I refuse to look at it. I have Dylan's voice in my head.

'Look them in the eye and make yourself tall.'

I line my body up in the direction where one shark is heading and dive down. Its milky white eye slides past. It has so many teeth that it can't close its mouth.

Milk

The sun is clawing at the window

The morning is cold

The cat is at the bedroom door

There's no milk in the fridge

Our son wants to play

You're not here.

    Yes, baby,

    Let's play a game

    I'll hide and you come find me

You're not here

You're not here

Nowra

On the road into town in late autumn the crepe myrtles burn red and orange. Above them is Cambewarra Mountain, the clouds hanging low around her face. For a moment, you'd think there's never been a town more beautiful. Then a man yells 'GET FUCKED' at someone just out of sight, startling the schoolgirls lying on the grass in their plain blue skirts, who sit up and then begin to laugh. Laughter is always a useful solution to fear.

Nowra is two hours from Sydney, give or take. It sits on high ground alongside the southern zag of the Shoalhaven River and at the end of the train line. The kind of regional town that people pass through on their way further down the coast. Or never leave.

It was built on the back of dairy and timber. Underneath the grime and fading shopfronts are the architectural lines of an 1850s town. In 1861, it had a moment of fame when Archer, a racehorse trained here, won the first Melbourne Cup. That was a long time ago. Today the boomer-rich live alongside the unemployed, and the town boasts an unemployment rate almost double the national average. Most of those who work in town have jobs in community services, or at the naval base nearby. But it's also home to young families, single mothers, musicians, and writers.

When George William Evans traced the outlines of this area on his coloniser's map in 1812, he described the country as 'broom scrub brush' with poor quality land for miles. The First Nations people he met gave him fine, fat oysters in exchange for fishhooks, tobacco, and tomahawks. If it wasn't for his Aboriginal guide Bundle, Evans likely would have died. Bundle built a canoe in half a day and ferried Evans and his troop of men across the Shoalhaven River twice. They kept walking. They tried to climb the Cambewarra Ranges and were stripped almost naked by the bush. As well as ruining his clothes, Evans cracked his ribs when he fell into the river on his way back to Appin. All the time he was taking note of what could be stolen, farmed, used. He wrote it down – tall trees, cedar. Red gold, property of the Crown.

Nara is how my phone transcribes the town's name from voice to text, an awkward record of my nasal Australian.

No – *w* – ra, I try again.

Nara, my phone transcribes.

Nao-uuu-rraaa

Nora.

The cedar-getters were already here by the time Dr Charles Throsby, surgeon and settler, came to the area on his last expedition south in 1821. By this time, Throsby had witnessed the violence and the atrocities of colonisation, and he was inseparable from it. He wrote a letter condemning the 'barbarity of our own countrymen'. Five years after this expedition south, he would commit suicide. *Nou-woo-ro*, he scrawled in his journal. A rough transcription of Dharawal language. Translated it means Black Cockatoo, or meeting place, some say.

Melissa says Nowra is a forgotten town. It was beautiful once, she says. She grew up in a fibro cottage on Jervis Street that her parents bought with the help of a war service loan, and lived there most of her young life, finishing high school in 1969. She remembers that the streets were once lined with giant Moreton Bay figs, camphor laurels, and tall Federation homes. That a country pub stood on almost every corner. There were farmers who came into town once a week on business, always dressed in their finest clothes; their wives competed against one another for best marmalade at the annual agricultural show. She remembers the church stalls and the girl guide badges. Her tennis lessons down on West Street, and how she would go the long way to avoid walking past old Meroogal House, which was overgrown and wild, always someone's shadow in the garden.

Every year she bought a ticket to the Sideshow Alley when it came to town, to see the bearded lady and watch a man swallow razor blades and swords. She snuck in to see Vanessa the Undresser, crowding into the tent with the men, who ignored her, watching the woman dance seductively before dropping her long, feathered fans.

On the verge of adulthood, Melissa got a job at Hewlett's Record Bar. It was the seventies. Woodstock and the Vietnam War had reached Nowra. Its counterculture politics drew a line through the town's respectable working-class values and gave the kids something to argue with their parents about.

I sink into Melissa's soft grey lounge and her old dog falls asleep at our feet as we talk. Books and art line every wall of her home. Photographs of her children, sketches. On the phone screen propped up in front of us is her childhood friend Jackie, sitting cross-legged in bed in Sydney. Now in their seventies, what they had wanted as teenagers was freedom. They rejected tradition and left home at a time when the popular options for young women in Nowra were debutante balls and, later, marriage and children. Instead, they moved into the ground floor of a grand Victorian house on Moss Street with two other friends. It was 1972 and the first all-female share house in Nowra at the time.

'I didn't want to get married, have kids, be a debutante. My father was devastated. I think he already had the frock picked out,' Melissa laughs.

I walk around Nowra more often lately, discovering new markets and cafés I didn't know existed. I wander by Meroogal House, now owned by the Museums of History NSW, and open to visitors interested in a house that was owned by four generations of women. I imagine the Thorburn sisters – famed spinsters – inside, writing one of their comical lists.

They huddle around the table in the sitting room at Meroogal, a home built for them and their mother by their brother Robert. Each week they used part of their weekly inheritance to pay him back. Kate raises the quill with a flourish: *myself*, she adds, laughing. It is a list of what makes a model woman. And in the column alongside, what makes a model man – *there are no such beings in existence*, one sister had dictated. *One who minds his own business*, another adds.

A good footballer and cricketer

No public school teachers: gents I mean

Homo est semper bonus

Man is never found good

Kate slips the list into the drawer with the others. Tottie Thorburn, the youngest, always likes these evenings together after a day well spent. This has been her home for two years now. With her sisters and mother, she has found peace in their independence. Maybe she was tempted to consider marriage once, when the young man carried her across the creek and waltzed with her somewhere in the middle, the water rushing at their feet. But that would have been a different life.

Today, she finished her work early and found her afternoon free. After tea, she played tennis with Kate, returning home together just before the sun set over the garden. None of the sisters are willing to give up their independence and this woman's house, with its rosebud wallpaper, for any husband. She and her sisters are paying their brother back and will one day own it themselves – the nicest house in town. Tottie sat at the piano and began to sing.

At Moss Street the girls smoked Kents and played Led Zeppelin loud, until the older French couple who lived upstairs banged on their ceiling to keep it down. People were always coming and going.

'There were a lot of drugs,' Jackie says. The dealer would come down in his blue Kombi, at first bringing marijuana. One weekend, heroin, which took some of their friends by the throat until they were in rehab or lost. But that was years later.

'When we left home, there was a lot of our lives that our parents didn't know anything about, and that we were unable to share with them. And it was probably the most important parts of our lives: who we were hanging out with, what we were doing, who our boyfriends were, who we were sleeping with – because, of course, we weren't supposed to be sleeping with anybody,' she laughs.

But something is happening and you don't know what it is. Do you, Mr Jones?

'It was called a *sexual revolution*, but that makes it sound like it was just about sex without any responsibility. Just a free for all,' Jackie continues. 'It was more love without ownership than sex without responsibility.'

'Yes, that you didn't need to immediately get married,' Melissa adds.

Jackie was seventeen and struggling behind the bra and girdle counter at Woodhill's under the glare of Mrs Cook and her white beehive hairdo. Melissa got her a job at Hewlett's Record Bar. It was a place to be seen, a foothold for the world outside. And they sold everything. Lottery tickets, tobacco and pipes, rifles, fishing gear, live bait; green weed and red worms you could hear sliding in their tubs. And of course, vinyl – a section of the shop managed by the coolest girl in town, who had recently travelled around Europe in a van and returned an authority on good taste.

'If you wanted to hear a new record, you came to Hewlett's,' Jackie says. It brought the young people who imagined a world outside the regional backwater.

Hewlett's Record Bar, like all the local businesses at the time, was family-run. 'The dads would do it and the sons would take over,' Melissa says. 'You couldn't walk down the main street without stopping fifty times because you'd see so many people you knew.'

The town had beautiful old houses and a bustling main street. Then the shopping centre opened across the highway, diverting customers to the new chain stores. A lot of the family businesses that had been in Nowra for generations went bankrupt or closed, including Hewlett's Record Bar.

'Nowra isn't like that any more. I walk down the street as fast as I can so I don't get shanked by somebody off their head on meth,' Melissa says.

That's Nowra now. The abandoned trolleys by the road. The graffiti telling passers-by someone loves them. The man who salvages cans from the bins and pushes his rattling trolley to the buy-back across the highway. The old woman, dressed in white, who removes her sword from its red and black sheath and dances with it on the grass outside the gallery. The kids riding their bikes fast down the footpath. Me, wishing they'd wear a helmet.

A woman, about my age, walks down the street and screams. 'FUCK!' At no-one, at everyone.

'This is what happens when you break someone,' she cries out. 'When you take my kids away.'

Everyone avoids her eyes. They look at the ground, the wall, the sky. Anywhere else. Nowra is known for it. In 2019 an enquiry into drug use found that of the fifty-two children removed from families in Nowra, 60 per cent were from homes where ice was being used.

Melissa, then nineteen, stood in Hewlett's and answered the policeman's questions. The woman had entered the shop and chosen the long dark rifle. She had seemed normal enough. A bit nervous. She came to the counter with the 22 and a box of bullets. Melissa rang it up, wrapped it, and accepted the woman's cheque, which would bounce later that week and get Melissa into more trouble. The woman left. She went home and bailed her husband up in the barn. She had tried to kill him for some private hurt, but the bullets missed.

'Probably deserved it, the bastard,' Melissa says.

I can't find an account of it in the newspaper archives. But there are other reports: a husband who slashed his wife's face with a glass; a thirteen-year-old girl raped and left for dead; a young mother who dropped her baby over a cliff; an Aboriginal woman murdered in town.

And just down the road there is the UAM Home for Aboriginal children. Melissa went there as a Girl Guide at about fifteen. 'I didn't know what they were there for. All these kids with snotty noses who just wanted to be hugged and carried around. Kids who had been taken and put into care, and they weren't being cared for. It was awful.'

How do I write this part? It can't be left out of the account, but I feel I'm not the person to do it. There was the ramping up, the meetings and marches, the fight for land rights. The mayor of Nowra at the time burning the Aboriginal flag in the car park (he's still on the council), the formation of Jerrinja Land Council, the closure of the UAM Home. I'm skipping ahead.

It's 1972 and four young women had moved into the share house on Moss Street. They were a band, a troop, an army. They protected each other. From prowlers who tried to break and enter at night (Melissa running down the street in the dark yelling and swinging a mirror at him). Ex-boyfriends who wouldn't take the hint (Jackie hiding in the cupboard until he left).

A dome of silence, that's how Melissa puts it. Which protected her when she fell in love with the girl who lived across the street and realised she wasn't straight.

'It wasn't even called that then. *Straight*. I didn't know what I was.'

In a small town where everyone was visible, the young women kept their relationship a secret. Or thought they did. It was on their faces, walking down the street. 'LEZZOS', someone screamed at them from a passing car.

'Did you enjoy your afternoon with your friend at the beach yesterday?' A snide remark from a man Melissa had known her whole life as he walked by one day. Who had stood out of sight and watched them.

It's getting late and Melissa's old dog is ready for his afternoon walk. I put my notebook and dictaphone back in my bag and make to leave. We start talking about other things.

'Where are you going to live? Will you stay in your house?' Melissa asks. She knows my husband left recently and it's just me and Joey at home. He wants the house.

'I might move to Nowra, I have some friends there.'

'Nowra!'

We both laugh.

The house on Moss Street was knocked down in the middle of the night. The workmen filled in the old well and put the highway on top. Progress came in four lanes and a new set of traffic lights. The girls had left by then. Jackie was in Darwin. Melissa had moved to Queensland but was already on her way back.

I drive over Moss Street and where the old house once stood. I'm on my way to an open house to find somewhere to live; a tiny fibro cottage that I might just be able to afford. Five of us gather in the front yard and wait for the real estate agent. She unlocks the door and smiles as we pass her one by one at the door. Inside, its walls are painted a sunny yellow, matching the original fifties kitchen. It has a flat suburban backyard and a garden shed. It needs some love – don't we all – but it's the kind of house where a woman might find her independence.

Blue umbrella

I found an umbrella on the train and took its small blue body with me.

How lucky to find one in all this rain! How intimate an umbrella handle is! How selfless! To turn its polyester cheek to the sky for a stranger.

I carried the umbrella toward Circular Quay. Passing children in raincoats with parents hurrying them along. I heard the buses hiss down Alfred Street. Saw the taxis inching along in the wet. The water pooled at my feet before running into the harbour and the South Pacific Ocean. It was the middle of the day, but it was already dark. Everything that was solid was melting away. Dripping and trickling. The rain kept coming. I was learning the strange ways that heartache and relief can live in the same body. The way it makes time pass in waves. And with it today, the shapelessness of the rain. It erases everything. Here we don't have shadows, only reflections.

As I walked towards the square sandstone building of the gallery, I saw a young blonde woman standing by the doorway waiting for someone. She held her phone up like a mirror, to fix her hair and makeup. Don't worry. You're beautiful, I wanted to tell her as I passed. But I had a feeling she already knew it. Who says that to a perfect stranger anyway? Only the ridiculous or the lonely would try it, and today I was neither.

The rain had driven more people than usual inside. They swung their umbrellas and stamped their feet at the door. Leaving trails of water along the floor and up the stairs. I checked my umbrella in at the front desk and took the small rectangular card offered in its place. We were a small damp crowd moving in concert through the rooms. Pointing and looking. Or walking grimly with our hands behind our backs. A young woman stood close to her mother in a short, pleated skirt and boots. A man slid his silver water bottle from out of his bag only to be reprimanded.

No drinking in the gallery! The attendant said.

Outside it kept raining, but we wouldn't know it. In here it was dry and lit.

I stopped in front of a work by Anne Samat. *Cannot Be Broken and Won't Live Unspoken #2* (2023). It ran up and over an entire wall in bright woven tapestry, reaching almost to the ceiling. In it, tiny toy soldiers hung by threads and plastic swords fanned out in elaborate detail. There were kitchen utensils and small bright beads. It was a work of immense patience. Described by the plaque on the gallery wall as a monument to family and friends that carried the artist's message of love. It was meant to wrap the audience in a hug, but it held me at a distance. I returned the card at the desk and was handed my blue umbrella.

I thought about all the umbrellas that change hands. That are left in forgetfulness and taken out of necessity. Scattered across cities. Hiding in corners or under chairs. There is nothing more patient than an umbrella. When the sun comes out, it will be folded neatly and forgotten again. Left leaning against a table at a café. Until it rains.

Oh look, an umbrella! Someone will say.

Take it, the rain will reply.

This is how it will find another hand to hold.

So it goes with us too. To be lost and then found. The small blue umbrella makes me think of you, even though I don't know who you are. Are you waiting for me? I'm not ready yet. But one day it will start to rain and I'll take you by the hand.

Let's run, I'll say.

And we'll go out in it together.

A few hours later, I'm in the doorway of my best friend's apartment with our arms around each other.

'You look better than I've seen you in a long time,' she told me. 'You have more colour in your face.' She raised her hand as if about to hold my cheek. It was true. The unravelling wasn't unravelling after all. I was sloughing off and straightening up. We stood in her kitchen where I kissed and tickled her baby's feet until she laughed. Two tiny teeth coming through. Big girl! You've grown! Her wide owl eyes. Her searching hands. All this change in one tiny body.

I hand myself over to their home. To bath time and dinner time. Nap time and play time. By morning, the rain has stopped. The sun gives the world back its shape. We push the pram in a circle around the park and avoid the long earthworms that have been drummed up out of the soil. The planes fly close by our heads. It's time to go already. We exclaim at the time. Already!

References

Women's time
Ideas explored relate to Julia Kristeva's essay of the same name.

Twenty-two pairs of sunglasses
'The conflict of familial life and creative identity', Rachel Cusk calls it. From her essay 'Lions on leashes'.

'It carries the recognition that we never really know our children, as Joan Didion wrote, partly because we can't see past our fear.' Paraphrased from *Blue Nights* by Didion.

The leather jacket part 2
Information about Minnie Quinlan accessed via the Blue Mountains Library Local History blog.

Some critics deny that Margaret Mead ever identified civilisation in a healed thigh bone, but it is a popular story that has been traced back to an anecdote shared by Paul Brand in his book *Fearfully and Wonderfully Made*.

Rabbit person
'I can't go on. I'll go on' is a quote from Samuel Beckett's novel *The Unnamable*.

Middle-life
'Now I understand that to love someone is to risk everything.'

Deborah Levy also writes: 'To separate from love is to live a risk-free life.'

Nowra
Sections about Tottie Thorburn and her sisters were possible through many hours reading the Meroogal House letter archives available via the Museums of History NSW website.

Thank you to Melissa and Jackie for sharing their stories about growing up in Nowra.

Acknowledgements

I would like to express gratitude to my family: Mum and Dad, Aunty Marl, and my two brothers, who I annoy and amuse in equal measure.

Thank you to my close friends, many of whom appear in this book. Some anonymous, others named. Jasmin, Amanda, Mandy, Lorien, and Ness – I feel very lucky to have the support of so many generous and intelligent women in my life.

Thank you Sian Prior for mentoring me as I wrote this book. You always encouraged me to dig deeper no matter how painful and showed me the importance of self-knowledge and courage in writing, among many other things.

Thank you Bonnie Porter Greene, for your support and permission to use your painting *The Pink Lichen Of The Sea # 2* (2022) as the book cover.

Thank you to my publisher Terri-ann White, for taking an interest in my work and guiding me through the publishing process.

Thank you, Joey, who has no idea his mother is a writer and that this book even exists.

And thank you Danny. For once in my life, I don't know what to write. I hope you already understand what I can't commit to words.

There are so many others. Thank you.

About Upswell

Upswell Publishing was established in 2021 by Terri-ann White as a not-for-profit press. A perceived gap in the market for distinctive literary works in fiction, poetry and narrative non-fiction was the motivation. In her years as a bookseller, writer and then publisher, Terri-ann has maintained a watch on literary books and the way they insinuate themselves into a cultural space and are then located within our literary and cultural inheritance. She is interested in making books to last: books with the potential to still be noticed, and noted, after decades and thus be ripe to influence new literary histories.

About this typeface

Book designer Becky Chilcott chose Foundry Origin not only as a strong, carefully considered, and dependable typeface, but also to honour her late friend and mentor, type designer Freda Sack, who oversaw the project. Designed by Freda's long-standing colleague, Stuart de Rozario, much like Upswell Publishing, Foundry Origin was created out of the desire to say something new.

Milton Keynes UK
Ingram Content Group UK Ltd.
UKHW041947131124
451149UK00005B/573